ALPHA MALE

the 7 Laws of
POWER

Mindset & Psychology of Success.
Manipulation, Persuasion,
NLP Secrets.
Analyze & Influence Anyone.
Hypnosis Mastery,
Emotional Intelligence.
Win as a Real Alpha Man.

Sean Wayne

© **Copyright 2021 - All rights reserved.**

The content contained within this book may not be reproduced, duplicated or transmitted without direct written permission from the author or the publisher.

Under no circumstances will any blame or legal responsibility be held against the publisher, or author, for any damages, reparation, or monetary loss due to the information contained within this book, either directly or indirectly.

Legal Notice:

This book is copyright protected. It is only for personal use. You cannot amend, distribute, sell, use, quote or paraphrase any part, or the content within this book, without the consent of the author or publisher.

Disclaimer Notice:

Please note the information contained within this document is for educational and entertainment purposes only. All effort has been executed to present accurate, up to date, reliable, complete information. No warranties of any kind are declared or implied. Readers acknowledge that the author is not engaged in the rendering of legal, financial, medical or professional advice. The content within this book has been derived from various sources. Please consult a licensed professional before attempting any techniques outlined in this book.

By reading this document, the reader agrees that under no circumstances is the author responsible for any losses, direct or indirect, that are incurred as a result of the use of the information contained within this document, including, but not limited to, errors, omissions, or inaccuracies.

CONTENTS

Meet Sean Wayne	ix
Introduction	xi

1. WHAT IS POWER?   1
Coercive power	3
Reward power	4
Legitimate power	5
Expert power	6
Referent power	7
Informational power	8
Where does the power come from?	8

2. ALPHA MALE POWER   11
Who is an Alpha Male?	13
Traits of Alpha Males	14

3. MINDSET AND PSYCHOLOGY OF SUCCESS   21
What is mindset?	22
What is psychology?	23
The Role of Mindset and Psychology in Success	24
Benefits of Having a Successful Mindset and Psychology	27
How to Develop a Successful Mindset and Psychology	30

4. MENTAL MANIPULATION   33
What is mental manipulation?	34
Stages of mental manipulation	35
Forms of mental manipulation	36
How do you use mental manipulation?	39
Benefits of mental manipulation	41
Effects of mental manipulation	43

5. PERSUASION	45
What is Persuasion?	46
How to Use Persuasion	47
Benefits of Persuasion	55
How to Develop the Power of Persuasion	58
Abusing the power of Persuasion	59
6. NEURO-LINGUISTIC PROGRAMMING	61
How Neuro-linguistic Programming Works	63
The Benefits Of Neuro-linguistic Programming	67
Neuro-linguistic Programming In Therapy	72
Concerns And Limitations Of Neuro-linguistic Programming	72
7. HOW TO FULLY ANALYZE AND INFLUENCE PEOPLE	75
How to Analyze People	77
8. HYPNOSIS TECHNIQUES	89
What is Hypnosis?	90
The power of the subconscious mind	90
How to use Hypnosis?	91
How to hypnotize someone?	92
Relaxation technique	92
Hypnosis in 5 steps	98
Benefits of Hypnosis	104
How to develop the power of Hypnosis	107
9. EMOTIONAL INTELLIGENCE	111
What Is Emotional Intelligence?	112
Principles Of Emotional Intelligence	113
How To Use Emotional Intelligence	118
Benefits Of Emotional Intelligence	121
How To Develop Emotional Intelligence	124
CONCLUSION	127
201 Positive Affirmations For Alpha Males	130
50 Positive Affirmations For Success	131
51 Positive Affirmations For Wealth	134

25 Positive Affirmations For Alpha Male Mindset	137
25 Positive Affirmations For Dealing With Depression	139
25 Positive Affirmations For Men: Anxiety	141
25 Positive Affirmations To Start Off Your Day	143

MEET SEAN WAYNE

Sean Wayne is a self-made Man, a graduate of International Relations and Diplomatic Science. He knows exactly what he's talking about because of his intense studies and his skills in relationships of all kinds. He is an authority on personality development because, to him, work, well-being, wealth, and love  relationships are not only an exact science, but also a noble art. Helping people achieve the next level of being a Man matters deeply to him, and what you're about to learn has helped plenty of Men gain the confidence to go after what they want. **Sean** is the perfect person to be writing this book as—thanks to his father's experience as a noted psychiatrist and his own psychophysical skills—he has become a guru of psychological manipulation, persuasion, and therefore... an expert in relationships.

His goal behind writing is to transform anyone from any background, social upbringing, and personal beliefs into a 100% Alpha

Male, left, right and center. And what better way to do this than getting into the psychology, habits, verbal and non-verbal language, charisma, self-esteem, vision, and tenacity of the Men who have it all. This book is presented by a Man who is an authority when it comes to being passionate and enthusiastic about the hows and the whys on how anyone can be an ALPHA MALE. No bullshit, no snake oil; just pure, hard facts that you may never have encountered until you picked up this book.

Above all else, the goal of **Sean Wayne**, in letting you in on his Bible of secrets and strategies, is to help you reach the pinnacle of your potential as a Man. His love for the topic and his willingness to share it with everyone who can benefit from this is a testament to just how much he wants everyone to resolve their deep-seated pains and inadequacies. His dream is that Men everywhere can have the opportunity to finally achieve the absolute pleasure they could only fantasize about - living the reality of a true ALPHA MALE.

INTRODUCTION

INTRODUCTION

Power struggles are an ongoing and continuous phenomenon whether you choose to acknowledge this fact or not. All Men make choices daily that impact and determine how much power they will have. Sometimes these decisions and qualities can be very subtle. You don't need to defeat the "Bronze Bomber," heavyweight boxer, Deontay Wilder, before you can become powerful. You can be powerful without being physically intimidating. This has caused many Men to ask how? This book will explain.

We are faced with decisions daily, and what you choose will show if you are powerful or not. Any Man who wants to be powerful must be ready to win his battles in all aspects of life. You might think I am exaggerating by calling it a battle, but it is a battle of the mind, emotions, knowledge, etc. If you want to have the best chance of winning this battle, you must prepare in advance.

This book has been written to teach Men how they can win this battle. It shows how power is expressed and how they can acquire and use power. This book has been written with real-life examples that any Man can apply in their lives if they desire to be powerful. Some may also ask *where* you use this power. The simple fact is that power is used everywhere around us, whether you admit it or not. In families, there are sibling rivalries; in romantic relationships, partners struggle for control. Workers compete to be the most powerful in their jobs. This book will teach you how you can use power in different areas of life. After all, why should you also not be able to use it? There's no good reason at all why you shouldn't. This book contains secrets that others have been using. I have written it in straightforward language that makes it easy for all Men to understand.

1

WHAT IS POWER?

Words Have Power

WHEN YOU SEE a Man in the gym lifting 242 pounds of dumbbell bars, you'd say that Man is powerful. If you witness a President passing a decree that no one should go out after 7 pm and the streets become deserted right on that deadline, you'd also say that the President is powerful. Power can mean so many different things to different people. Power has various specifications in many walks of life. A sociology expert, for example, might define power as the ability to influence the decision of others.

If you conduct research and ask people what they think power is, you could come back with twenty definitions. That's why I say the definition of power is relative. Your definition of power can be influenced by what you are thinking about, what you have experienced in life, what you want to do, your desires. It could even be something as simple as wishful thinking.

Let me give you an example of different ways that people can define power. One of my favorite scenes in the hit television series, *Game of Thrones*, was when Cersei challenged Lord Baelish's definition of power. He believed that power is obtained from knowledge, but she showed that power is also having direct control over others. She demonstrated this by telling her soldiers to arrest him, even though he'd committed no crime. She released him shortly afterward, but she'd made her point. In this particular instance, his power was weaker than hers.

Actually, they were both right, depending on circumstances. Power could be knowledge, and power could be influence. All that matters is the situation of deployment. The covid-19 pandemic led to the death of millions of people, and some are still dying. If someone successfully produces a cure for it, he or she can be classified as the most powerful human on earth because they have something that everyone wants. This is another type of power.

Power is a very important aspect of human civilization, and the desire for power is ingrained into the mindset of most humans. Power could be political, societal, physical, social, or academic. As I have explained, there is no universal definition for power, but it's usually an exertion of authority, influence, and control over others.

For a better understanding of power, we can divide it into five classes which I will now go through:

Coercive power

Have you watched a movie where someone is being held at gunpoint or being threatened by a knife? Perhaps the person with the weapon is trying to make the other person do things they don't want to do? This sort of power is known as a coercive power, and it works by the use of fear. But you can show coercive power without the use of a gun or knife. For example, a brother threatening his sibling to do something for him because he caught the sibling doing something wrong on video. In other words, the brother is using blackmail. He is threatening to expose his sibling's secret.

This can be used in an organization where the fear of losing a job or being demoted can trigger a positive or negative response. A positive response could be an employee who is struggling to carry out his task. Suddenly he gets a burst of energy and completes it quickly before his colleagues have finished their work. It can also be negative because most threats are on the borderline between motivation and bullying, and it could swing either way, depending on who it's used on and how it has been used. This happens because the source of this power is problematic, and it can quickly be abused. If it is abused, obviously it can cause harm to people around. This can be seen in blackmailing cases where someone holds some evidence of guilt and makes the other individual do his bidding.

I would not advise you to use coercive power in a professional setting. Quite apart from the moral questions, it rarely produces a positive outcome in practical terms. It would most likely end up in a bullying claim or, at the very least, a miserable environment for workers.

Reward power

There are many manifestations of power, and you can use the power you have to force or direct someone towards compliance. Here you use the power of reward to attract an individual. A popular example of this is depicted in children all around the world when parents tell kids to clean their rooms, do their chores, and do their homework, and they'll be rewarded with candy. And, of course, every year there is the promise of good children getting presents from Santa Claus.

Candy is unlikely to work for adults, but there are things that adults want that can encourage them to comply. Examples include bonuses, increases in pay, training opportunities, tickets to sporting events, and sometimes a thank you. You can use this power by creating excitement and making your workers and colleagues motivated about the reward. You can do this by triggering the part of the brain that loves being rewarded for work done.

While using the reward power, you should know that you can run out of things that you can give to people you are trying to motivate. If they are encouraged by financial reward, you won't be able to give them money at every turn. A good way to use reward power for adults is to give them public thanks and praise; it will also act as a source of motivation for others. If you say excellent things about people that are doing well in the company, it can make other employees want to be praised. Sometimes these other workers aren't normally among the people that are being praised. But if they see others being praised, it can encourage them to do better and get their share, as well.

If you want the use of monetary rewards to be very significant, you should make sure that they do not happen often. Keep them only for special occasions or major achievements.

Legitimate power

This is much like the example I mentioned earlier where a President passes a decree, and it is enforced because he has the power. This kind of power comes from the position of an individual. It could be a CEO, governor, police chief, or anybody who's a recognized authority.

A power that stems from this post does not remain with the person and would leave the person once he or she is out of the post. The unstable and unpredictable nature of this type of power shows that it is solely dependent on the position. The power obtained comes from legitimate sources such as electoral mandates, social hierarchies, organizational structure, and cultural norms.

The source of this power allows the person that is wielding it to make decisions about areas where his power is accepted, but they would be ignored if they meddle in situations where they do not have power. A police chief can ask for your identification, but he cannot declare a curfew because it's not within his control. The President of Russia can make rules that affect his country, but he cannot decide how other countries will behave.

In an organization, legitimate power means that you are holding an important position in the organization. You could be the boss or an important member of a leadership team. The power instilled in key members of the organization will be felt when you are in contact with other members of the organization. This power also gives you the ability to enforce changes in the organization. It also allows you to monitor the compliance of the people that work under you.

The effect of legitimate power will be properly felt if there is a clear chain of command in the organization or society.

Expert power

You can also accumulate power from your experiences, skills, and knowledge. The knowledge that you acquire from years of experience and practice makes you skilled and authoritative in that area. Your skill gives you power because your opinion about several issues would be considered when decisions are to be made. Your opinion is valid because you understand the situation, and you provide adequate solutions from a clear and solid viewpoint.

When your opinions regularly outperform those of others, people will learn to trust you, listen to you and respect what you have to say. Being an expert about something can make you a leader, and it confers a kind of power on you which comes only from a wealth of knowledge.

Expert power doesn't just impress people who have witnessed your skills. Your qualifications can also make people call you an expert. This power can even be used by people who are not experts as long as there is a perception of expertise around them. The power that you get from being an expert does not last forever, so you have to keep improving if you want your opinions to remain valid. I would also advise you to entertain the opinion of others when making decisions, even if you are an expert in that field.

Referent power

In this technological age, this is presently the most used popular form of power. Many celebrities are idolized, and their opinions influence a lot of people. The referent power comes from the post or status of an individual. People that wield this power are often seen as role models to others, and their opinions are trusted and respected.

This power can be observed in social media, where the words of people with a huge fan base can even determine how an election will turn out. This power can influence small and huge decisions. This power can be obtained from skill, knowledge, talent, or family. Sometimes you are just *given* the power because a set of people have found you likable and have decided to listen to your opinions.

This can be used in many walks of life. It can be used in organizations. Have you ever wondered why someone who is on your level is more respected? Other people seem to warm up to their opinions much more quickly than they do yours? This could be due to the power of being popular, friendly, confident. This kind of power could be acquired by just being nice to people.

Similar to every other type of power, power comes with responsibility, and you must be careful not to abuse the power that you have. Many people with referent power get power-drunk and start using it to publicize hate. You should know that just as quickly as you have been given that power, you can lose it likewise. The people who value your opinion can decide not to stop respecting you. Many people throughout history lost their influence when they stopped being responsible.

If you want to be a leader, it is not enough to have referent power from fame or other trivial sources. You should also have knowledge in abundance. A leader that has both expert power and referent power has a greater chance than someone who has one or neither.

Informational power

This kind of power does not last forever, and it is classified as short-term power. This power only exists for a brief period when you know something that everyone else does not know. Unlike other types of power, informational power does not necessarily confer influence or help you to build credibility. For example, you could be a project manager who has been given information about a project, or you are responsible for making decisions about how the project will be carried out. During the duration of the project, you have power because of your position and the information you possess.

It is difficult to hold on to this type of power because you will eventually have to release the information that gives you the power. This type of power is less useful for leaders because of its brief duration.

Where does the power come from?

There are many theories about the origin of power; some believe that power comes from an acquisition. They believe that the only way you can have power is if it's given by another individual or entity. This theory comes from the view that power is a position or title that is given to an individual. Such individuals believe that the title an individual acquires gives them authority and control over others.

There are some people that believe that true power can only come from within. Their own perception about the origin of power comes from the school of thought that power comes from the capability of an individual. They believe that the power of a person is influenced and enhanced by the choices they make, their actions, and how they think. Here, the real power comes from the inside out, and this determines how strong you will be.

Some religious folks also believe that true power comes from God. Some scientists believe power comes from the application of science. It is also not wrong if you say that power comes from the economy of a country or military prowess. Just as there is no one definition for power, there are also many origins of power.

If you go into a school and ask a class of fifty students about the origin of power, there would be different answers. The differences do not mean most are wrong. In fact, most of them would likely be right; the differences only occurred because we all think differently and because we define power differently.

My definition of power is also different. I believe that power is the ability to exercise influence and control over others. The organizational chart does not matter much to me as I believe power is available to anyone irrespective of position or title. You just have to be ready to wield it. There is power everywhere, but many lack the courage to wield it. In this book, I will be talking about the power I wield daily and how you can also employ it if you desire. This power comes from inside me, and I can also teach you how to generate power and influence from yourself.

In this chapter, I talked about what power means to me and where it comes from. In the next chapter, I will emphasize how power can originate from Men.

2

ALPHA MALE POWER

THERE MIGHT NOT BE enough time in a day to do the things that you want, but one thing that the world has in excess is diversity. One of the aspects of life's diversity is our personalities. There are various personality traits in Men and women, and many of them can depict how we will react to situations.

There are many traits in Men, and the numbers differ, depending on which study you consult. Here, I will mention six, and they are:

- Alpha Male
- Beta Male
- Gamma Male
- Omega Male
- Delta Male

In this book, I will focus more on the Alpha Male. Earlier, I told you that power is available to anyone that is willing to wield it. I have successfully weaponized the power in me, and it has greatly benefited me. The ability to use the power embedded in your personality is something anyone can do if you put your mind to it. I was not always bold, confident, and fearless, but I was determined not to let fear dictate my life.

I was tired of the girls I liked walking past me without my being able to say a word. Whenever I was able to summon the courage, it would always end with the girl laughing in my face as I stuttered. My only relationship with someone I liked was always the Friendzone, and it made me hate myself deeply. I watched the girls I liked in relationships with Men I admired. I wanted to experience what it felt like to voice my opinions without fidgeting. I wanted to stop doing things I hated because I was scared to speak up.

This attitude that I displayed did not only affect my relationships; it affected other areas of my life. My self-confidence was heavily affected, and I became a prisoner in my own self as fear took the reins. My only saving grace was a thought in the form of a question which was - is this how all Men live? The answer is NO, as I have found out. My success story started when I discovered the power in the Alpha Male personality and started weaponizing it.

The personality traits that you exhibit as an Alpha Male can provide you with power and influence.

Who is an Alpha Male?

The term Alpha originated from the Greek alphabet; it is the first letter. The meaning of alpha has gone beyond being the first letter since its adaptation into English culture. Alpha is now commonly used to denote dominance. A popular example can be seen in wolves, whose hierarchy is denoted by Greek letters. The leader of the pack is called an Alpha wolf which means he is the leader. He's the strongest and most influential as all decisions and mating rights belong to him. This is portrayed in many movies and series.

It is not only used in animals. The traits that humans show are also classified with these letters; as I explained earlier, this works for both genders. Just as we have Alpha wolves, we have Alpha Males who exhibit leadership traits, are successful, and are at the top of the socio-sexual hierarchy. This kind of Man is admired and desired by most Men and women.

You might not like the fact that personality traits determine how you are viewed by society but let's face the fact that although we are all humans of the same species, we are still different. These differences come with traits and a form of power. In this chapter, I will be talking about the power that Alpha Males have. There is no denying the fact that Men who depict the character traits of Alpha are often the most desirable, and most Men want to be like them. If you want to exhibit the kind of power and influence they have, you need to understand where the power comes from. Some Men are born as Alphas, and some become Alphas.

Traits of Alpha Males

What makes some Men Alphas is not the size of their biceps and triceps or how attractive they are. It is based on the things they do. Here are some of the characteristics that Alpha Males exhibit.

Acknowledge their flaws

Contrary to the opinion of many that Alpha Males are perfect, that is very untrue. No one is perfect: all Men have flaws and Alpha Men are no different. You might have been told that Alphas are god-like creatures in the shape of Men who are confident in every area. But that's false. Alpha Males are not extremely confident in all situations, and there are times that they might not act like the complete "macho" Man you think they are.

In such situations where their flaws are apparent, they do not shy away, hide their flaws, or pretend they do not exist. They're honest about them - they would rather acknowledge them. The ability of a Man to acknowledge his flaws makes him different from most Men and people in general. This trait makes them stand out amongst other Men. One of the things that Men try to avoid in relationships is their significant other finding out about their weaknesses and flaws.

The truth is that hiding our flaws stems from confidence and self-esteem issues. These issues make such Men afraid since they are scared of their partner or friends finding out they are human. This is because having flaws makes you human; it does not make you stronger or weaker, you are just human. Alpha Males know this, and they are not scared to acknowledge their fears in front of people.

When you acknowledge your flaws, you are taking power from anyone that wants to use them against you. The ability to be confident irrespective of your flaws makes you powerful and you can use it to your advantage. Men who do not let their weaknesses and flaws control them are always in charge of things around them because once you are confident in yourself, the things that appear as impossible to you seem far less of a challenge. When others notice this, they will respect you; their perception of you changes. The respect you have gained increases your influence and your power because not everyone has the courage to do what you did.

If a Man allows his flaws to dictate his dos and don'ts, his confidence and self-esteem would be affected. That will be very visible to people around you, irrespective of how you try to hide it. Some hide their flaws and weaknesses in the form of anger, and they are always defensive when they feel people are catching up to them. I personally am scared of heights which many might see as a weakness, but I am not ashamed to tell people.

Face inner fears

It is normal to be scared of some things, and every Man has something that he's scared of, but you can only overcome these fears if you confront them. You should know that most of the problems you face daily are caused and created by fear. Another thing that many do not know is that those fears are irrational and not real.

You could be scared of being picked on, judged, and laughed at by others, but so is everyone else. I know it's not a good feeling if people are laughing at you or making fun of you because of what you said, wore, or did, but it is not the end of the world. We all have problems, and most people will quickly forget the thing you did yesterday that made them laugh. Sometimes it might not be immediately, but they would get over it soon or move on once something else comes along. You should also know that people care more about their own fears and insecurities than they do about yours.

I mentioned earlier that I am scared of heights, and I even sometimes scream when it gets too high! I can even remember one date where my girlfriend at the time wanted us to go to Disneyworld and try the Pixar Pal-A-Round. I screamed throughout the ride, and some people laughed at me, but I did not care. You might also be laughing, and I don't blame you, but heights just happen to be my personal fear. I've no doubt that everyone else has fears of their own.

There are many fears that we face daily, but our reaction determines the kind of Man that we are. The difference between an Alpha Male and other Males is that the Alpha focuses on conquering his fears rather than running from them. The Alpha nature of a Man is not dependent on one action but rather all the actions in a day. Each day we take a journey filled with fears; the success of a day determines how many of those fears you are able to face and conquer.

An Alpha can have moments within the day where he does not give off the Alpha vibe associated with Alpha Males, but at the end of the day, he would have faced more fears and taken more risks than other Males. People think once you tell people what you're scared of, you become undesirable. That is completely false. Take my example again; if a woman thought less of me for being scared of heights, that's no problem; it wouldn't affect me, I'd just move on. There is a possibility I might never get over some of my fears, but I am okay with that too, and I would rather focus on other things that make me an Alpha.

I mentioned earlier that Alphas are successful, and the ability to face their fears is one of the reasons why. There is a kind of power that is attached to being successful, and once people see how successful you are, your influence increases.

Take charge

The direction of your day is determined by the decisions you make. Many Men are scared of taking action, or they do not trust their decisions. You might think that it is very simple to make a decision and stick with it, but it is not. Sticking with a decision that you made, means that you are accepting responsibility for whatever comes out of it, be it positive or negative. How many of us regularly stand by our decisions?

Your daily progress should be based on how many of your decisions you stood by. Don't be scared of failure so much that you become a passenger in the car of your life. One thing that is peculiar about all Alpha Males is that they trust themselves and stand by their decisions. This does not mean that they do not accept help from others, but they trust in their abilities to be successful.

The best way to live your life is when you are in control of the affairs of your life, no matter how scary the decisions you have to make are. No one knows you better than you; if you want to experience the power of an Alpha Male, you cannot take a passive role in the affairs of your life. Practice this in all you do, and if someone else gives you a chance to make decisions for them, show them you have the ability to take charge. It could be a friend or a partner. Show how Alpha you are in those situations and enjoy the power of an Alpha Male.

. . .

Know when to stop

Alpha Males know when to leave things alone, which is contrary to the popular belief that Alpha Males are arrogant, aggressive, and are always looking for opportunities to show brute strength. Alphas are not erratic, and they do not fight over random things. Power does not come from beating everyone around you for no reason; a powerful Man does not always need to clench his fists before you know that he is strong.

Alpha Males are not boastful thugs like people often think. In fact, usually, they are calm and rational individuals. You do not have to exaggerate little things or become violent over irrelevancies, and people who do that are probably trying to compensate for the lack of something. Remember that a king does not crown himself. Men who fight over everything are just insecure, and they use violence to hide their insecurities. Such Men can start fights because of how you look at them. They're trying to prove a point, but they're just showing how foolish they are.

The difference between Men with Alpha vibe and others is that they know when they should stop and leave things alone. You do not have to escalate any argument or be involved in bar fights to make a statement about yourself. As you go through life, you will be in situations that make you angry and meet many people that will try to make you annoyed. People that derive pleasure in making others angry are usually angry about something else. Most of the time, it is about their own problems; they are just trying to deflect the anger onto you.

Alpha Males are great at risk assessment, and they can quickly determine if a situation is worthy of a conflict or whether they can leave it alone. This does not mean that you should be scared of confrontation, but you should avoid unnecessary conflicts. For example, if some people try to rob you when you're walking home, you can decide to fight back. But if you are fighting because someone accidentally spilled your coffee on you, it's hardly worth throwing punches. It would have to be the perfect Starbucks cappuccino with a little foam on the top to make a fight worthwhile! Jokes aside, if you want to enjoy the power of an Alpha Male, you shouldn't make a fuss over trivial issues. Alpha Males know when to pursue things, when to leave them alone, and when the reward outweighs the risk or vice versa.

The power of an Alpha Male in an intense situation is to calm down and settle disputes amicably if it is possible. Or just to leave it alone.

Internal competition

You might have heard that Alpha Males thrive in competitions. This is true, but they often prefer to compete with themselves. Alphas prefer internal competition because it provides them with an opportunity to improve, which is their sole reason for competing. Social media has made it easy for people to pretend, and if you are focused on competing with them, you will keep losing. Instead of allowing yourself to lose an unwinnable battle, focus on making yourself better.

Each morning, the first thought of an Alpha Male is how to improve based on his performance from yesterday. He's usually not interested in unhealthy competition with Harry on Facebook, who claims to live on a yacht but really has no home. The Alpha Male prefers to improve by an inch daily than keep losing to fakes like Harry. This is because losing affects your confidence. An Alpha Male should be confident, but once you enter into the wrong competition, you start to lose your Alpha vibe.

The right competition fills you with power, desire and keeps you motivated as you embark on an improvement journey. As you keep improving, the power you carry by being an Alpha Male will only increase, which will improve your confidence and self-esteem.

3

MINDSET AND PSYCHOLOGY OF SUCCESS

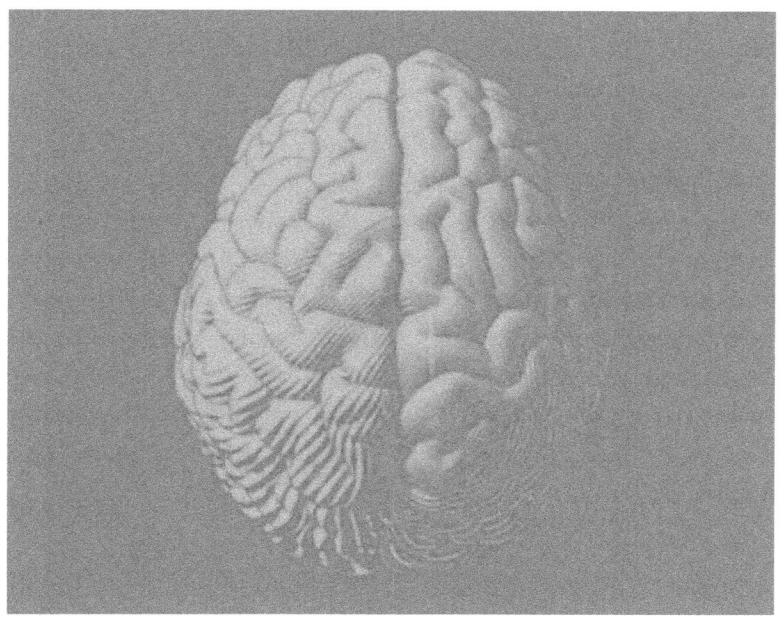

IT IS everyone's wish to be successful, but not all wishes come true. Many Men do not become successful because it takes more than throwing a coin down a wishing well or hoping that Santa

Claus magically grants you success. If you want to be successful, you must be ready to work for it. We all have goals, no matter how old or young we are. They could be small or big. The goal of a teenage boy might be to date the most popular girl in high school, while that of a grown Man might be to become the President.

The actualization of these goals or dreams is a success. You should know that not all goals are actualized, and only the goals you are ready to work for will become accomplished. Goals are like children, and you are the parent. Sadly, not all parents who gave birth to a child ten years ago still have that child today. Some children could have died from illness, gun violence, or hunger. Most of the things that cause children to die can be prevented, but not all. As a parent, you must make sure that you do your part to protect your child and give it all it needs to survive. The goal is your child, and you are the parent.

Sorry for going dark on you for a minute; I'm sure you get the gist. Jeff Bezos, Elon Musk, Mark Zuckerberg, Joe Biden, Barack Obama are all successful Alpha Men, but they did not just become successful because they had a dream. There were many things they had to do to become what they are. In this chapter, I will talk about some of those things - mainly, the mindset and psychology of success. If you want to be successful, you must wield the power of both a successful mindset and psychology. Although they are similar in meaning, I will discuss them separately.

What is mindset?

Mindset broadly refers to the way people think about themselves and the world in general. Your mindset is formed by the things that you have thought about and how these thoughts affect the way you think and form your opinions. Do you think every guy thinks the same way? The answer is no, which is why there are differences in our mindsets.

There are two major types of the mindset-growth and fixed mindset. Men with a fixed mindset believe their fixed traits determine their limitations and success, and these things cannot be changed. If you have a fixed mindset, it means you believe that effort is not required in the battle for success. Just as the name suggests, Men with the growth mindset believe that there is room for improvement for those who are persistent.

A growth mindset suggests that you can develop your abilities and talents if you desire and are ready to work for them. Suppose you believe that anyone who is persistent and determined enough can become more talented or smarter. Although Men that have a growth mindset believe that improvement is possible, they also know that some people are born geniuses like Mozart, Da Vinci, or Einstein. They know that trying to achieve such levels might be impossible, but it does not stop them from trying.

What is psychology?

Human beings have thousands of thoughts every day, and they all stem from the mind. The mind is a very powerful part of our human make-up. You will have heard the saying that someone is lost in thought. This means that someone is thinking so deeply he becomes unaware of what is going on around him. The mind is so powerful it can control the other parts of the body. It also affects how you relate to things.

The possibilities of the mind make it paramount to understand how it works. Psychology is the study of the mind and behavior. It also takes into accounts the factors that affect how humans think, act, or feel. Examples of such factors can be biological influences, and social and environmental factors. If you want to understand the actions of people, go deep into their psychology, and you will find the reasons. There are many aspects of psychology such as social, cognitive, developmental, personality, etc.

The Role of Mindset and Psychology in Success

Success starts with the mind, and if you want to be successful, you must be able to harness the power of the mind. Your mindset and psychology will be responsible for a major part of how successful you will become. If you want to be a successful Man, you cannot afford to think like every other guy or act like other Men. Your behavior and your thoughts must align in the pursuit of success. The mindset and psychology of successful people differ from that of others. The mindset and psychology of success is one of the laws of power that will be discussed in this book, and it is essential for all Alpha Men. An Alpha Male must be able to channel the power of their mind to propel them to success.

The mindset and psychology are part of our subconscious mind. The subconscious mind is very powerful, and it takes a huge chunk of your brainpower. It is responsible for most of the functions of the body, including memories. Even though most of the actions performed here do not need the body to be aware of them, you can take control of this area and make it work for you. Once you are able to take control, you will be able to align every part of your brain, including your mindset and psychology, to achieve what you want, which is success. There are also other ways that you can use to make your mindset and psychology work for you.

Visualize your success

One thing that has limited many Men from achieving success is vision, and not everyone is capable of visualizing success because of the things it requires. Visualizing success means that you must be strong in the face of fear. You must be courageous enough to picture success even when everyone has predicted failure. These qualities are attributes of an Alpha Male, and they are what make Alpha Males successful. If you want to channel your mindset and psychology into being successful, you must create a mindset that reflects the kind of ambitions you are aiming for. The mind is a very powerful tool, and the way you decide to use it will determine the kind of result you will get. Success is never accidental and you will have to deliberately work towards it. If you are able to create a successful mindset, success becomes achievable since all your thoughts and behavior will be focused on it.

Meditation

An Alpha Male does not relax after creating a vision; he continues to channel the power of the mind towards achieving the goal. Alpha Males know they have to take actions towards success despite having a clear vision. One of the things that impacts the amount of success a Man would have is the ability to attract success with his mind. If you want to use the power of your mindset to attract success, you must find a way to connect with your mind. Meditation is renowned for being a great way to get in touch with your mind. Meditation brings you closer to your mind; it helps you to channel many mindsets towards your goal.

Be willing to see change

If you want to use the power that the mind produces effectively, you must be ready to change. Change does not start with your actions; it begins when you start to believe that it is possible. It is not an immediate process, but you must take the first step, which is the desire that things can change. You can practice this by trying something that you think is possible. Change does not happen by sitting idle and folding your arms. It happens when someone makes a conscious effort to achieve it. Successful Men are not held back by the state of things because, instead of their minds thinking of the negatives, their minds are focused on how they can bring change. If your thoughts, actions, and behaviors are channeled towards a goal, not only will you be the first to be successful, you will have the power to actualize change.

Negate fears

The reactions of people to different situations speak a lot about the way they think and their behaviors. People who react negatively to different situations are only trying to pass on their fears to you. Use the success mindset that you are cultivating to block out the noise from such people. Alpha Males must learn to control the type of thoughts they allow into their minds. For example, if you are getting married and you decide to share the news, there would be two types of responses. Some would be happy for you, and others would treat the news like a funeral. The people who tell you to enjoy the rest of your life as a single person are only displaying a failure mindset, probably due to their inability to conquer their fear of marriage and commitment. If you have a positive mindset, things like that should not disturb you.

Identify the resistance

An Alpha Male should understand the power of his mind; it can make him successful or a failure, depending on how he chooses to use it. Our minds are capable of having positive and negative thoughts simultaneously. If your mind is holding you back from doing the things that you like to do, it is because there are some resistances in your mind. Having a successful mindset does not mean there will not be internal and external resistance on your path. Instead of letting that resistance hinder you, identify it, and find a way to overcome those resistances as you proceed. Your success mindset enables you to persevere when others would not.

Be open to possibilities

You can use your success mindset as a way of protecting and strengthening yourself when things don't go according to plan. If you have a goal to create something new, you should not fold your hands in defeat if your first attempt fails. You should rather start thinking of new ways that you can use to actualize your goals. The success mindset allows you to quickly recover from losses because you believe in yourself and there are always new opportunities and possibilities.

Benefits of Having a Successful Mindset and Psychology

The mind of a Man is his strongest weapon if he knows how to use it well. Being physically stronger does not guarantee your success, and, as I have explained, an Alpha Male does not go around showing his physical strength; he lets his mind do the talking. The power of the mind of an Alpha Male comes from his mindset and psychology. There are many benefits that you will enjoy from having a positive mindset and psychology. They are:

Happiness

Most successful people are happy. This statement might be different from what you have been told, but you should know that success means different things to different Men. A Man might consider a day where he is able to eat a three-course meal a successful day, while another Man might consider a day where he made one million dollars less than ideal. This is because goals are different. Men that have the right mindset for success - a growth mindset - are happy with what they are doing as they take each day as a chance to improve. Once you have a successful mindset, taking on new challenges will not be a burden to you as it is just a chance to use the power in your mind.

Improves your self-esteem and confidence

There are many studies that have shown that Men are bad at identifying their abilities because of the way they think. This inability affects the self-esteem of many, and it costs some their chance to be successful. However, the power of a successful mindset allows you to think highly of yourself and does not make you settle for less. Once you have aligned your mind with success, you will be able to know your strengths and weaknesses. Before I had a successful mindset, I considered myself a failure, and I let the abusive words that people spoke to me affect me personally because I was mentally weak. I got into unnecessary fights because I wanted to prove my strength as I thought that was my power. When I harnessed the strength of my mind, I discovered I was doing many things wrong because I wanted people to validate me. I stopped doing those things, and I focused more on the power of my mind, which helped to boost my self-esteem.

Improve your relationships

Some relationships have already failed before they start; let me explain. Men who are not strong mentally tend to self-sabotage their relationships unknowingly because they came into the relationship with a wrong frame of mind. The failure of their relationships is only confirmed at the start of the relationship. People think only animals can smell fear, but this is very untrue. The stench of fear in some Men can be perceived from miles away. If you see a girl that you like and the first thing that comes to your mind is you are not good enough for her, that relationship is likely to fail because you will always be insecure.

At work, if you see yourself as weaker than other guys and you think they are cooler than you, it might be impossible for you to become their friend. This is because if you eventually approach them, you will talk to them like they are your boss. That attitude will hinder your chances of being their friend or partner. If eventually you miraculously become their friend or partner, that feeling does not leave, and you will most likely do anything to keep them as your friend, irrespective of the personal cost. Such Men lose themselves in the relationships, and once your friend or partner smells this, the relationship is likely to fail. Alpha Males do not think of themselves as inadequate. They overcome any fears they have.

Ready to improve

The fear of being deemed stupid stopped many Men from learning new things. Like it or not, you cannot be perfect in everything that you do, and you will need people many times to help you get through. This fear comes from the mind as such Men already think of themselves as failures. They think asking questions will make everyone think that they really are failures. Successful Men are not scared to ask questions that others could laugh at as long as they know that will improve their knowledge. The inability to focus on improvement is not found in many Men, but all Alpha Males exhibit it. Once again, it stems from the mind. Once your mindset is focused on success and you think like a successful person, what people say about you tends to matter less. The weak mindset of some Men could be as a result of early failures that they think classifies them as a loser. This is totally untrue. You should not be overly concerned about occasional failures; they should never define you.

How to Develop a Successful Mindset and Psychology

If you want to enjoy the benefits of a successful mindset and psychology, you must have it. You should know that success is not an act but a way of life. Here are some ways that you can use to develop it.

What does success mean to you?

Earlier, I mentioned that what is considered a success is relative, and before your mind can reflect success, you must determine what success means to you. Start by creating goals for yourself. They should have a clear plan and a way you can gauge the progress of these goals. You should also know that even if you fail to meet the first goal, you are not a failure. Just keep trying until you are able to succeed in all the goals you have set for yourself. Have a positive attitude when you experience setbacks and see them as opportunities to learn. This kind of attitude will make it easy to overcome small failures with your zeal intact. Do not be the kind of Man that makes everyone around you miserable because you experienced a setback; that sort of attitude will drive people away. If you want to be an Alpha Male, you must learn to keep a positive attitude when things are good and when they are not.

Follow your gut

People think that all success stories are products of a calculated decision after careful evaluation of data. This is very untrue, and Men who believe this would only stay on the same point with the same mindset. Success takes confidence because in your life, you will be at a crossroads where the next step might be blurry, and you need to make a decision. In such a situation, you either ask for help or follow your intuition; the answers to some things are not always calculable. Following your gut instincts, irrespective of the result, will improve your confidence about your abilities and create a belief that you have what it takes to be successful. It will help you make good and firm decisions.

Take action

If you want a mind based around a framework of success, you must be productive with your thoughts. Do not just make plans about your goals; be ready to take action on those thoughts. Many Men do not take action because they are scared of failure. Alpha Males are not scared of failure, and if you want to be an Alpha Male with the power of a successful mindset and psychology, you must be ready to fail. We have all failed in the past and might still fail in some aspects of our lives and careers, but the reaction to those failures is what determines how your mind will be. The quicker you can turn ideas into goals, the easier it will be for you to make progress that improves your mindset.

Take responsibility

A successful mindset means you are able to accept responsibility for the outcome of every decision that you make. You should be prepared for the possibility that not all your decisions will produce a positive outcome, and you will have to deal with some failures along the way. When you cultivate the habit of taking responsibility, you become more resistant to failures. If you make a wrong decision that affects someone or your reputation, accept the blame. This helps mitigate the damage and it will maintain your reputation. It will also act as a learning opportunity on how to avoid such mistakes in the future. It will not always be a negative outcome, and when you accomplish something, you should also take responsibility. This will make you understand that you can be successful, and it will support you on your path to more success.

Affirmation

The things that you listen to have an effect on who you are. Suppose you have a success mindset and enrich your mind with things that will either motivate you or people around you. The success mindset will help you to attract the right people. The power of affirmation cannot be overstated. It strengthens confidence, belief, and it acts as a confirmation that you can be successful.

In this chapter, I talked about one of the laws of power, which is a trait of Alpha Males. The mindset and psychology of success provide power to Men. They can utilize it if they know how to. I will focus on another law of power in the next chapter.

4

MENTAL MANIPULATION

WE ARE NOW MOVING into the second law of power, which is mental manipulation. Here we will talk about another way to harness the power of the minds of others. Like I said in the previous chapter, the mind is a Man's most potent tool, and it is vital that all Men make the best of it. If you have control over your mind, you will have a better chance at success, and if you have control over the minds of others, you become a manipulator.

Before we get into mental manipulation, let us determine what manipulation means. Manipulation is a tactic that can be used by Men who are incapable of saying what they want directly, and so they resort to unhealthy strategies. Manipulation can be emotional and physiological, although they are related. Since the mind controls how you think, it affects how you relate with others. Hence, we can say that every form of manipulation starts from the mind. There are different forms of manipulation; some can be easily detected while others are difficult to spot.

What is mental manipulation?

Mental manipulation is the process of modifying a person's beliefs, thoughts, attitudes, and behavior by deceptive actions for personal gain. The people involved in manipulation are the manipulator(s) and the party being manipulated. If you are being manipulated, it is unlikely you will realize what's happening because you surrender your free will to the manipulator. Anyone can use or become a victim of mental manipulation.

For example, let's say a crime was committed by a big firm; it could result in millions of dollars in damages if they lose the resulting legal case. If the firm wants to preserve its image and unlawfully win the case, it can look for weaknesses in the people involved and blackmail them. This can be done by paying witnesses to commit perjury if they need money. It might even involve kidnapping loved ones of the judge and jury so as to manipulate their decisions.

You might think that making someone do things they do not want to should be easily spotted by the victim, but this is false. Mental manipulation often occurs in stages until it forms a cycle, and the cycle keeps on repeating. Manipulators are frequently clever at gaining trust, and only then do they show their selfish and controlling side.

Stages of mental manipulation

The manipulation often starts in a friendly and good relationship. The first stage is always favorable to the victims because the manipulator is still looking for weaknesses. Have you seen a documentary about lions stalking a wildebeest, waiting for the right time to pounce? This is similar to what happens in a manipulative relationship. Here, the predator and the prey are not far apart and would be near each other.

In those documentaries, the lion plans to trick the wildebeest into moving in a direction where it thinks it is safe, but which is always a trap. Here the trick is to become close to you so that they can find your weaknesses and exploit them. This is the second stage. The manipulator looks for your psychological vulnerabilities and decides on the most effective tactic that he will use based on the vulnerabilities he's discovered. You should also know that a mental manipulator is willing to cause harm to his victims directly or indirectly if necessary. Very often, such people are relatively unbothered even if they do cause harm.

Mental manipulation is very exploitative, abusive, and deceptive due to the complete and utter disregard the manipulator has for his victim. Sometimes the victim will even make excuses for the manipulator, thereby allowing the situation to continue.

Clearly this type of manipulation is deeply dangerous. It's not the kind of situation any sane person would want to see happening. However, by understanding how it works, an Alpha Male can use milder forms of manipulation to get what he wants without doing harm.

Forms of mental manipulation

Mental manipulation can take different forms based on the choice of the manipulator.

Reinforcement

Reinforcement is the use of a tactic to modify the behavior of an individual. The aim of reinforcement is to increase the chances of something favorable happening. Alpha Males can use this to increase their influence. There are two major types of reinforcement - positive and negative reinforcement. Both types can be used by Alpha Males.

Positive reinforcement

You might have heard this phrase from parents to their children in a bid to make them do the things they want them to do. It could be promising them candy if they finish their homework. This can also be done with adults, although perhaps not with candy. For example, your boss might promise you a raise if you are the best employee at the end of the year. The additional incentive to completing a task is positive reinforcement. You can use this as a form of mental manipulation if you discover you are working with someone who likes receiving gifts, no matter how small.

You can also use this in relationships by promising your significant other something they want if they do something for you. You should do this covertly to avoid disputes with them, but it can also be done openly if the reward is sufficient. A covert example is if you let it appear unplanned. You should not make it obvious that you want it. Make it look like they want it. If you want to avoid some engagement, you can promise her a Birkin bag if she agrees to exclude you.

Negative reinforcement

Similar to positive reinforcement, where you will promise something as motivation. Here the motivation is to avoid losing something. You should know that loss can be good and bad. For example - your boss promises to remove one query from your files if you do something for him, or he could add a query to your file if you do not do something for him. Your partner could threaten to take your PS4 away if you continue to leave the house messy. The fear of losing the PS4 will prompt you to clean up. Instead of letting people use this mental manipulation skill on you, find out what they don't want to lose and use it to get what you want. Alpha Males should understand how to use the right type of reinforcement in different situations.

Mind games

Mind games are covert, coercive attempts, often pretending to be innocent communications, designed to manipulate an individual or individuals. The intention of the manipulator is simply to keep confusing the victim, which will prevent them from discovering the true goal of the manipulator. Some mind games can, of course, be playful, but most of them are dangerous. For example, for those who watch sports, players say things to each other to get into the minds of their opponents. Coaches say something to the press when they mean the exact opposite. For those that watch soccer, you would have heard about Jose Mourinho; he's notorious for doing this.

There are other places where Men can use mind games other than in sports. For example, you can use it in relationships to shift the blame onto the other partner. The connection between the manipulator and the victim will affect how deep the mind games will be. If you are in a committed relationship with someone who is using mind games on you, it would be difficult to detect. The difficulty stems from the unrivaled trust between the two of you because some of the tricks used look normal. Mind games can be used in many forms, which will be explained below.

Guilt trips

Here the goal of the manipulator is to make you feel guilty even when you have done nothing wrong. This is very common in romantic relationships. Suppose you catch your partner cheating and confront them about it. They try to make it look like the reason they were cheating is because of your inadequacies. They could say, "I cheated because you were neglecting me and coming home late all the time." But they neglect to mention that they encouraged you to take a job with a lot of traveling involved because of the better pay rate. Most victims of this form of mental manipulation eventually end up apologizing, even after they have been wronged. Manipulators can be very skillful at turning the tables and making the victim feel guilty.

Although it is very pleasant to see someone committed to the things of God, some partners also use religion to guilt-trip others. They may use religious virtues to make you feel bad about things. Religion is a personal decision, and, while it has many positive attributes, it should never be forced down the throats of others. Guilt-tripping with religion is when your values are judged based on the religious principles of others.

Such partners would make you feel you are the cause of the things that are wrong in the relationship when you are only trying to help. It is important for Men to understand how this form of mind game works in order to overcome it. This leads me into the next form of mind game.

Confusion

The manipulation does not stop after you have apologized to your partner. That's because such occurrences will not only happen once. You will become confused and start doubting if anything you say is even true. For example, you could see her kissing another guy, and she will tell you they only shook hands. Normally this would be hard to believe, but the picture that will be painted will make you doubt your vision. This is where the degree of relationship comes into full effect. The trust that you think is present in the relationship will make you doubt things. That's because when your partner successfully makes you see things from only their point of view, you start to lose yourself.

You will start questioning your thinking, and, soon, you will not be able to make decisions for yourself without informing them. This is when the full power of mental manipulation is felt. You will believe anything he or she tells you. You should know that mental manipulators do not care about the pain or confusion of their victims. In fact, some enjoy it. Men who fall prey to this form of mind game are often left as shells of themselves and deprived of their Alpha nature.

How do you use mental manipulation?

The aim of manipulation is control. The manipulator and the victim are in a struggle over the mental control of the victim. Have you been in a situation where you lost control, and things started going haywire? For example, imagine driving a car without steering. How does it look to you, and how do you think that will end up? Control is a very powerful force among humans. One of the reasons why some Men become religious is because they want someone else to take over the reins of their life. In this case, a divine power.

The power of control gives you additional abilities. You will be able to dictate, influence decisions, and direct the movement of others, provided you have control over them. The ability to exert control over others is not to be taken lightly, as no one likes to be controlled. If you are being controlled by someone, you lose free will and the ability to make decisions for yourself without outside interference. You should also know that there is a need for a kind of control in the world as long as it does not rid you of your free will.

However, mental manipulation rids you of your free will because it aims to control thoughts, emotions, and behavior. Men can use this power after they understand the person they are trying to manipulate. If you want to manipulate people mentally, start by building a relationship with the person. There are many forms of mental manipulation; the relationship you have established should give you a good idea about which one would be effective. The most effective mental manipulation is one that can last for a long period of time and can give unrestricted control.

As you experience an increase in control, the victim would start to lose their grip on reality as you shred their sanity piece by piece. Mental manipulation can be very powerful, and the victim would start to experience shame, guilt, and low self-esteem. The results of mental manipulation are never the fault of the victim. Just as you can manipulate others, you can also be manipulated, and I can tell you it is one of the worst feelings.

The human mind is structured and designed to work on self-motivation and freedom. These feelings would be directly impacted by mental manipulation. If you are being manipulated, it would mean surrendering access to those feelings to someone else's control.

Benefits of mental manipulation

Although this power is often used negatively, it can actually be used to do some good. All of the benefits of mental manipulation favor the user. Alpha Males can use this power and enjoy the benefits it brings. I will explain some of its benefits to Alpha Males.

You get what you want

Any Man who is able to exert this type of power on someone else will get anything he needs from the person with ease. If you can manipulate your boss, you can ask for raises which would be quickly approved. You will also enjoy other unique benefits which would attract the envy of other workers. You can also manipulate your partner to do things for you that you do not like to do. For example, I have never been a fan of going to stay at my girlfriend's father's beach house, but we always go there for Thanksgiving. I was always stuck there with poor reception and Wifi, and I hatched a plan to avoid it. Some weeks before Thanksgiving, I said that her favorite band was coming to a town not far from us. I told her that Tony at work had front row seats if she wanted, and she agreed to go. This was how I started skipping those uncomfortable dinners with her dad. It does not have to be huge like this; you can use it to avoid doing dishes and to have uncontrolled access to alcohol, especially beer.

Help others make the right decisions

This is a good use of mental manipulation. This gives Alpha Males a way to coerce friends and partners into making the right decisions that they do not want to make. Sometimes this could be down to pride, laziness, etc. For example, let's say you are a partner in a struggling company that needs finance. You eventually find the money, but it turns out the help is coming from a former relationship partner of your business partner. Due to the history between your partner and his partner where he was cheated on, he decides to cancel the talks because of his emotions. You can mentally manipulate him to see what is best for the company. It could also be in your romantic relationship where your partner has been dilly-dallying on a decision that would benefit her. You can choose to take the decision into your hands and manipulate her into taking the opportunity.

Clearly, you have to be careful when doing things like this. You should know that regardless of the intention of the mental manipulation, even if it's a good one, you are still taking the free will of the person you are manipulating.

It becomes a tool for you

If you are able to exert this on anyone wherever you go, it is an additional tool you can whip out and use when necessary. Evaluate the situation and choose the form of mental manipulation that fits perfectly.

Effects of mental manipulation

You might have seen some people completely ignore reality and become a shell of themselves without realizing it. This is one of the results of mental manipulation. The mind is a powerful weapon, but it is also fragile and must be protected from harm internally and externally. When people surrender control to someone else, it affects them in all their functions. I have seen people lose control and go into a downward spiral in their level of confidence and balance (emotionally, physiologically, mentally, and socially). Some start suffering from low self-esteem and mental health issues. This kind of internal chaos makes me feel for them.

I often have the urge to shout at them, tell them to stand up to it, and take back control. If I did, I'd be doing that to try and restore their sanity, but I know the cause for people's problems is not always easy to pinpoint, and shouting would not solve it. Some effects are short-term, while others are long-term. Individuals that cannot regain control would struggle to maintain relationships both personal and professional. Such individuals would find it hard to trust, which would make others hate and be defensive toward the manipulator even if the intent was positive. When you are dealing with control, it is essential to have a balance, especially when it is someone else's mind.

In this chapter, I have explained the important things that Men should know about this law of power. Here, you will find the definitions, benefits, how it is used, effects, etc. With this chapter, all Alpha Males should be able to master this law of power, and also if and when to use it.

5

PERSUASION

HAVE you wondered why your co-worker always seems to get what he wants and you don't? Have you wondered how your girlfriend has made you do things you did not want to do? Whether you have or have not, I will tell you how they have been doing it.

It's not a difficult method to understand. You just have to know what it is.

What is Persuasion?

Daily there are decisions that Men have to take; some might be favorable while others might not. Just as you have decisions to make, so does everyone else, and those decisions can affect you positively and negatively. The ability to influence the decisions of others to favor you is what I call Persuasion. You should know that Persuasion does not have to be to the detriment of others. Nonetheless, there are things that a Man can do to influence the behavior and attitude of others towards him.

Your co-worker and your partner that I mentioned earlier are already using the power of Persuasion. Persuasion is often carried out by effective communication. Communication here is not limited to the things that you say; For example, if your romantic partner asks you to do something for her and you refuse, she can give you the silent treatment until you accept. The attitude displayed by your partner has communicated what she wants, and, most importantly, it persuaded you to give in.

Here, effective communication is what triggers the response; you can call it a stimulus. The response is the change in decision, attitude, or behavior. Before Persuasion becomes effective, the first thing to do is communicate what you want. You should add additional information in a manner understandable to the person you are persuading to improve your chances of being successful. Persuasion is only effective insofar as the influence that it has on its recipients.

If you want Persuasion to work, your audience must surrender to its influence. Your audience can also agree to it and be ready to effect these changes. An effective persuasion must be able to last long enough in the minds of your audience to allow them to act on it if it requires a long-term action. If the impact needed is immediate, it should be able to trigger immediate actions. You should know that the aim of Persuasion is to make your audience execute the behavior implied by new changes to the attitudinal position. This skill can be used by Men if they know how.

How to Use Persuasion

Reciprocation

Have you wondered why some Men do not like receiving gifts from everybody? In fact, some do not collect gifts at all. Human relationships have shown that people tend to help people that have helped them before. This unspoken rule probably started during the initial evolutionary period of Man. Cooperation has been used as a method of survival, and it is still in use now, just differently. You might have heard this saying, "You owe me one," which means one person is indebted to another. Whenever you give someone something, or someone does something nice for you, there is an unspoken I owe you one or vice versa, as the case may be. This is the law of reciprocity that makes people feel indebted to people that have done something good for them.

You could also have heard the saying, "You scratch my back, and I'll scratch yours." When someone owes you something, you have power over them, whether you or the person acknowledges it. Cooperation in humans works in a way that when someone does something nice for you, it creates an urge where you feel you have to reciprocate. The need to reciprocate creates a power void that can be utilized by Men. If you want to use the power of Persuasion, you must be a source of helpful information and positivity.

Just as there is an unwritten rule that Men feel the need to help people that help them, you should also know that there is a human tendency to dislike someone for being a regular source of bad news even if it wasn't caused by that individual. You will not be able to utilize the power of Persuasion if you are disliked. You might notice that many Alpha Males arouse hostility in others, people sometimes feel that they're too proud. This kind of dislike is mostly envy, and, secretly, many would want to be you if they see you as an Alpha Male. You can use this in your workplace by presenting gifts to some of your co-workers. Start with people you talk to as it will be very difficult to exert any kind of influence on someone you have no relationship with. Make sure the gifts are thoughtful and something they can appreciate.

You can also surprise your partner with something that they want and then notice how they start acting towards you. I have tried it many times, and it works, and many times, the night ends up with me getting lucky. I'm sure you get the gist.

Social proof

The immediate environment and the world at large have an effect on Men everywhere, whether you choose to accept it or not. Many studies show that people laugh longer at sitcoms that have laugh tracks than those that do not. Some might doubt this as I did, but I tried with my favorite comedy series of all time, *The Big Bang Theory*. You can also try like I did by watching one of your favorite episodes; I was unable to pick a favorite. I played the episode with just closed captioning and I was shocked that I did not laugh much; I just didn't find it that funny. I realized that if I had watched all the episodes that way, I would have had a very different view of the series. I could have even chosen another show as my favorite; it could have been *How I Met Your Mother* - so you see the fate I was lucky to avoid!

Why do you think the brilliance of Johnny Galecki and Jim Parsons was unable to make me laugh? The answer is very simple. The way we view things is influenced by how others see them. The degree of a behavior or situation is partially determined by how others react to the situation. You might have also noticed that when you are in an awkward situation, you tend to look around the room before you respond. It's almost as though you're checking what others will think of your response. No one wants to be the odd Man out. Following social protocol would help you avoid more mistakes and make you seem like everyone else. Unfortunately, that's one of its disadvantages.

Persuasive power as a result of what I call "social proof" cannot be denied, and it can have an effect on your work, relationships, etc. For instance, your partner could ask you to do something because others are doing it and the urge to look normal overcomes your confidence and boldness. People that are skilled in the art of Persuasion can use the idea of social proof to manipulate decisions. You can also use the power of Persuasion in your job. If you are working in sales, you can tell customers to buy a product by telling them that everyone is buying it and that it is the norm. If you can successfully convince others to do something that they do not want to, you have started utilizing this power. It's a power that's not only available to Men. Other genders can use it on Men. You should ensure that this power does not work on you. Ensure that you do things because you want to and not because of others.

Commitment and consistency

One of the desirable traits that a Man can possess is consistency. Alpha Males have this attribute, but it is often used against them. However, Men can also use it on others if they know how. Another way Men can use the power of Persuasion is by using the words of others to move their own agenda forward. For example, when people say yes, they are bound by their word, and most people would not want to go back on their word. They would rather do everything within their power to ensure that their word is meaningful. In a bid to save face and maintain the consistency of their word, you can use that power over them.

The need to be consistent with the things that everyone says is deeply ingrained into the culture of all humans. It has something to do with "saving face," and most Men will have tried to protect their image at different moments. One of the reasons why Men do this is to avoid the fear and shame that is associated with people who are inconsistent. You might have heard some of the terms used, such as wimp or wishy-washy.

The fear of those words being used against people can be utilized by Men to persuade them to do things that they do not want. For example, you can want a friend to say yes to a proposal to work together. You can invite him to a get-together and decide to make the toast. During the toast, you announce to everyone that your friend has agreed to work for you. At that moment, he will not be able to say no, and the fear of being labeled a wimp would make your declaration work.

Men can also use the foot in the door technique. The technique involves influencing others to say yes to some small requests, which can be followed by bigger requests. This technique is effective in large gatherings. Men can also profit from the commitment and consistency principle by reminding someone of decisions that they might have made in the past. That can help persuade them to take your side. You can do this by reminding them of past decisions that were similar to yours and encourage them to make the decisions again. For example, if you want to take a paid vacation from work and your boss has denied you, you can go up to him and remind him of the paid vacation he gave Ted, Jake, and James and cajole him to also grant you the leave.

You should also know that just as Men can use this principle on others, it can also be used on Men. An Alpha Male should understand this power to use it and also identify when someone is using your past decisions to promote their present decisions. If and when it occurs, you can be like me and tell them that different circumstances warrant different responses. For example, your partner might ask for a car from you, and point out that you bought one for your last girlfriend. She could even say it could be because you do not love her the way you loved your ex. You might be shocked by that, but I am not; I have heard it all. She is only trying to persuade you even though it is toeing the line between Persuasion and mental manipulation. It is good to get gifts for your partner, but you should not do it because you did it in past relationships.

Liking

Men who have been to an Avon sale or pyramid scheme offering would have experienced the use of this form of Persuasion. Many are not aware, but we tend to say yes to people that we know and like. This trick is commonly used by sales reps by saying your name again and again to create a false sense of familiarity and relationship. If you are wondering if it works, it does, and I have been a victim, especially if the person is physically attractive. Do not beat yourself up too much about it; I also did not know about it until I understood the laws of power.

There was this particular convenience store where I always bought more than I needed - like, who needs ten cartons of cereal? But I would always buy more to impress the beautiful attendant whenever she said my name, told me I was cute, and asked me if that was all. In order to impress her, I would always say no and buy more. My sense would finally come back hours later when I saw what I bought and how much I spent. You should know that receiving compliments from people and finding certain similarities between yourself and others can persuade you to make a decision. You should also be careful and ensure that others do not use this technique on you.

Authority

The authority that Alpha Males exude comes in handy here. Studies have shown that people tend to respect the opinion of credible experts. Men who are experts in a field attract a certain amount of respect from people, and others will also pay more attention to that kind of Man. For example, Dr. Terry Dubrow and Dr. Paul Nassif are certified experts in plastic surgery and they appear on the reality TV series, *Botched*. People would believe what they say over other unknown doctors.

This strategy is used often in sales as people tend to buy things endorsed by experts in that field. This is often used by athletes because people are likely to buy more performance-endorsement products if it is promoted by someone perceived to have superior physical skills. For example, if Stephen Curry endorses a product he uses to train, that product would experience increased sales. The use of authority to persuade can be employed in many areas.

For example, there was this guy, Tony, who I knew at work. He wore very nice Nike sneakers; his opinion was recognized and taken as law when it came to shoes. If Tony turned around and said that your shoes were knock-offs, everyone would believe him and would make fun of you for wearing something fake. His words were never doubted, even if you had proof to the contrary. He also had this persona that made you believe him, coupled with the fact that he was a loudmouth who liked to banter too much. Take that, Tony! - that's for saying my Nike Air Force trainers were knock-offs.

The power of Persuasion under authority stems from the fact that people trust authorities. It is very easy to trust an expert's opinion; it removes the burden of having to make tough choices. Sometimes the decisions we make might be wrong, but if they were based on someone else's opinion, it is easy to shift the blame onto them. Just like every form of Persuasion, it can also be used on you. If you want to protect yourself from the influence of unreliable authorities, you must try to deduce what the authority gains from it. If you deduce that it would only be profitable to them, take your mind off it. Ability to deduce such unspoken advantages will ensure you are not swayed by their words.

Scarcity

You must have heard that as the offer ends at midnight, you should be among the lucky few to get this precious commodity. There are only a few pieces left, do not miss out on this rare opportunity and call within the next 15 minutes. This is a common tactic employed by shopping channels, commercials, and shopping platforms, and they are effective. Things that are scarce tend to have more value in the eyes of humans and even more so when we're told that the commodity is different, unique, and special. These terms are sometimes synonymous with scarce.

The effectiveness of scarcity to persuade comes from the ability to create a sense of competition with others. This false sense of competition motivates people to get it because of the joy they will feel if they own a scarce commodity. Men can use this by making others believe they will lose something if they don't get it. The possibility of a potential loss plays a trick on the mind of humans, and it influences their ability to make decisions. Studies have even shown that people are more motivated to avoid loss than they are to gain something of equal value.

This principle above is how a Man can use the power of Persuasion via scarcity. Alpha Males can use this by emphasizing the things that others will lose if they do not do what you want. For example - your partner loves antiques and she has been asking you to go to a museum with her, but you have always refused. If you want to get the latest PlayStation, you can tell her you will go with her to the museum with her if she gets it for you. If she says no, you can start describing how memorable the experience will be if you go together. Emphasize how much fun the experience will be for both of you. You could even promise you will spend the whole day there, although I do not recommend it from experience. I was very bored! If she is still uncertain, create a sense of urgency and tell her the offer ends tonight.

You can protect yourself from this principle by carefully analyzing situations to see if you are being rushed into a decision. If you have made the decision, you can take a step back to decide if you want to continue with the decision.

When you want to use any of the forms of Persuasion listed above, you should make sure that you pick them based on the situation at hand. You should think carefully before adopting any form of

Persuasion into your current setting. If you are able to carry it out, not only will your power and influence grow, you will also become more resistant to these strategies because you will recognize them easily.

Benefits of Persuasion

If you are wondering if Persuasion is beneficial to a Man, it is, and here is why. Persuasion is a law of power that is neither good nor bad; it is just power, and the kind of Man you are determines how you use it. Persuasion can be a gift, and here are some of its benefits;

Self-expression

One of the things that you will enjoy as an Alpha Male is influence, and Persuasion allows you to increase your influence. Studies have shown that influential Men have better chances of expressing themselves than others. Any Man that is able to make others see things from his point of view has started to exert influence over others. This power helps Men build their self-esteem. As you become an influential person, you'll start to see this.

Considerations

One of the aspects I listed earlier about Persuasion is commitment and consistency. This doesn't mean telling lies to trick the mind of the individual. All you have to do is relay facts transparently and honestly in a way that will benefit you. If you are able to influence the decisions of others by stating only facts, it shows that you have what it takes to be a leader. People that can convince others to do something by effective persuasive communication are more productive at their jobs. Once people notice this power, they would start considering you for leadership positions in your workplace and in society.

It becomes a tool for you

If you want to make the power of persuasion work for you, you must become better at it. If your prowess in Persuasion improves, you have a better chance at persuading people. The power of Persuasion enables Men to be able to study the environment and situations to come up with different strategies and methods that they can use in various situations.

Productivity

If a Man is able to exert influence over others by Persuasion, it will increase his chances of being productive. For example, a Man that has persuasion skills and works in sales can use those skills to bring more money into the company than others. What you should know is that a lot of people that come into stores do not know what they want. If you are working in that company, you are an authority on the items in your care, and you can use that to your benefit and tell the customer what products are better, even if it's more expensive. If you can convince them, your daily productivity and monthly productivity increase.

Improves Relationship

Relationships are a major part of life, and Alpha Males understand this fact. The power of Persuasion is also beneficial for Men in different kinds of relationships because it helps Men to be able to relay their feelings to other parties involved without losing charge of the discussion. For example, if you are in charge of firing, increases in benefits, contract renewal, etc., in a company, you will have to tell people bad news on occasion. The best way to do this is by having a great deal of communication savvy which you can get by effective Persuasion. If you want to fire someone, there are two ways that Men can do it with Persuasion. The first is by relaying the news to an audience by facts and logic. You can do this by telling the employee that if we do not close this department in the company, many other departments will follow.

The second way is by persuading the person emotionally. You can do this by emphasizing that this decision was not taken lightly and that the company had to do it because it could affect others. You can also tell them that if they accept this difficult decision, they will help thousands of people that will struggle to provide for their families. The continued emphasis will show them that the decision was necessary.

There are some cases where Men must not attempt to persuade another person. For instance, this applies to a romantic partner in a relationship; you shouldn't attempt to persuade them to have sex - NO means NO. This does not mean you cannot persuade them to do other things for you if it will not be disadvantageous to your partner. Any Man who is able to persuade his partner by doing nice things for them will become happier and enjoy healthier relationships. Persuasion makes it easy for Men and their partners to make difficult decisions in their relationship.

How to Develop the Power of Persuasion

If you want to become a successful persuader, there are things that a Man can do to increase his ability as a persuader. They are;

Build relationships

If you want to be able to persuade others, you must have excellent people skills. Before you can think of being a persuader, you must improve your ability to have effective communication with people, mostly in a friendly manner. If people cannot bear the sight of you, it will be almost impossible to be a good persuader. You also must be able to understand, empathize with others, and build trust, sometimes agreeableness. You must be able to build productive relationships with people at work, at home, and in society at large. Most of the people you will use your persuasive skills on are the people around you. Even if you do not use persuasive skills on them, it is good to have interpersonal and emotional intelligence skills.

Build your confidence

It is impossible to convince someone else about something if you are not confident about it. The power of Persuasion helps Men to build their confidence because you will have to be confident to successfully persuade others. If you are an Alpha Male, Persuasion is one of the powers that you will be using daily without batting an eye. Alpha Males find it easy to communicate with others and can express themselves clearly. You can become more confident in delivering persuasive speeches by practicing them in advance. Remove all non-verbal signs that make you look nervous.

Practice your communication skills

Another thing that a Man can do to improve his persuasive skills is improving his ability regarding how he talks to others. Work on developing how you communicate professionally and personally. You can do this by making an intentional effort to be aware of all conversations and interactions you have with others. When you are working, find a way to start a conversation with your colleagues or join their discussions. A common conversation starter among Men is "Did you catch the game last night?" If you are not a sports guy, find something others have in common with you and talk about it. You can also make a conscious effort to contribute to group decisions and be involved in meetings at your workplace. Make sure you maximize any opportunity that can improve your communication skills; it will equip you to become a more persuasive speaker.

Abusing the power of Persuasion

The power of Persuasion can be beneficial, as I have discussed earlier. But it's true that Persuasion is a tactic that can be used negatively as well as positively. Here I will focus on how the control provided by Persuasion can be abused by Men. The abuse of this power is mental manipulation. Men who abuse this power try to create a mental prison for others. This abuse starts because the people using such persuasive skills want to gain more control of their audience at any expense. You should only Persuasion to help your audience understand why your opinion could serve them better or why they should support you.

There is a thin line between Persuasion and mental manipulation, and some users do not know when they have started abusing. An example of abusive use of Persuasion is when you convince your audience that there is only one way to see a situation, and that is your way. In order to create this view, you modify the truth and tamper with their reality until the victim has no other choice. After forcing them to see things only from your viewpoint, you proceed to manipulate them to act accordingly. Men that abuse this form of power often do it in isolation because isolation breeds desperation which they finesse to their advantage.

Not only do Men who abuse this form of power create an alternative reality for their victims, but they also make them believe that it has been the victim's decision all along. Some say things like, "This is what you wanted, stop pretending." They could also hold it over someone and say, "I did not force you." If you are using Persuasion to confuse people's reality or you coerce them till they lose sight of what is real and what is false, then that becomes manipulation. This is because the victims have started creating their own mental prison. Your persuasion skills are starting to disintegrate their core identity. History has shown many examples of dangerous leaders who've managed to do this.

In this chapter, I have discussed how you can use the power of Persuasion and the benefits that it offers successful users. You should also know that this form of power can be abused. It is essential that all users pay attention to why they're employing Persuasion and who they're using it on. In the next chapter, I will be talking about how to analyze people successfully.

6

NEURO-LINGUISTIC PROGRAMMING

MARTIN WAS a young lad of just seventeen years of age when he first witnessed a physical fight between his parents. The violent situation continued for several months, and it led to his parents' divorce. This divorce had a negative impact on him, and he began to exclude himself from the rest of his family. Martin began to perform badly in school due to the fact he couldn't concentrate. His results worsened, and he had to be transferred to different schools to revive his academic studies. He eventually graduated and went to Canada for his first degree. At the age of thirty, Martin was having difficulties in securing a well-paid job, and he had no intention of ever getting married. He was finding it difficult to stay committed in relationships. All the women he encountered tended to abuse him emotionally. His self-confidence and worth were affected, and he felt he wasn't good enough most of the time. In a bid to find a solution to his predicament, Martin went to the internet to get help, and fortunately, he stumbled on the page of a certified Life Coach and trained Psychotherapist. He booked an appointment with the coach after reviewing the coach's page. During the course of his sessions with the coach, he was able to deal with his childhood trauma, past experiences and started the journey to healing, forgiving, and letting go. At one point, the coach applied Neuro-Linguistic programming methods. This was due to the fact that Martin had some limiting beliefs and barriers that were affecting how he chose women, his self-esteem, and his life in general. Different coaching was introduced during the course of the healing in order to move Martin from his damaged state to a place where he felt much better about himself and life. He is currently in a relationship that is healthy and he and his partner are starting a family. Believe me, Martin wouldn't have been where he is today if not for the help of the life coach who made use of various tools, including Neuro-linguistic programming.

Neuro-linguistic programming is a method of altering someone's thoughts and behaviors to help achieve a positive outcome for them. It is a program that carefully studies thoughts (Neuro), Language (Linguistic), and the scripts which our lives run through (programming). NLP is focused on understanding and developing the mind. NLP is based on understanding the language of the mind, how it has been designed to function, and how it has been molded by our personal experiences. In simple terms, it is the study of subjective reality.

Since NLP began in the 1970s, its popularity has risen enormously. It's a psychological approach that makes use of analyzing strategies that have been used by successful individuals and employing them to reach a personal goal. Neuro-linguistic programming combines thoughts, language, and patterns of behavior gained from experience to achieve specific outcomes.

Proponents of NLP are of the opinion that all human action can be viewed positively. Therefore, if a plan fails to materialize or the unexpected happens, the experience of such a situation is neither good nor bad; they believe that it presents more information that is useful. Today, a wide range of fields are making use of NLP, including counseling, medicine, theatre, art, sports, law, education, and the military.

Richard Bandler and John Grinder were the brains behind the development of NLP; they are of the opinion that there is every possibility to identify the way a successful individual thinks and behaves and for others to learn these mental habits.

How Neuro-linguistic Programming Works

The three key elements of Neuro-linguistic programming are modeling, action, and effective communication. It is always believed that if one can understand how a task is accomplished by an individual, the process can be replicated and passed on to others so they can achieve success in a similar task.

Proponents of this method suggest that every individual has a personal map of reality. Practitioners of NLP analyze theirs and other perspectives to develop a chronological overview of one situation. The best way NLP users acquire information is by understanding various perspectives. Those that belong to this school of thought believe that senses are important for processing information that is available and that the body and mind have the capacity to influence each other.

The approach of Neuro-linguistic programming is experiential. As a result, if a person is to understand an action taken, such a person must undertake such actions too, so as to learn from the experience.

Advocates of NLP believe there are natural hierarchies when it comes to learning, change, and communication. The six levels of change are presented below:

Spiritual purpose: this is related to involvement in something that is larger than oneself, such as ethics, religion, or another philosophical system. When it comes to change, this is the highest level. With regard to purpose and spirituality, such things have minimal connection with anything material; they're less concerned with issues such as careers or where you want to live. Rather, it is about developing a set of values, principles, and beliefs that makes life more meaningful to you, and then you use these beliefs, values, and principles to guide the decisions and actions you take. Finding a spiritual purpose is contrary to what many Men think. Most Men measure how well they have succeeded through the vocation they have learned and their methods of finding money. However, finding a spiritual purpose makes you take a higher view. The question all Men should be asking themselves to achieve spiritual purpose is; what does it mean to be a good Man? You question the purpose and meaning of your life; how can you connect better with others? What is the best way for a Man to live? While there are numerous means that can help you find a higher purpose, it is typically a quest that can take a lifetime. Interestingly, Neuro-linguistic programming is a means that can help every Man to achieve that life-long goal.

Identity: when it comes to identity, you have to perceive yourself the way you want to be, and this includes one's responsibilities and the roles you play in reality. There is always this idea of what we all want to be like. For instance, you might want to be a public speaker who stands in the presence of a crowd and gives a speech with boldness and firmness; this is who you see yourself as in a perfect world, but, in reality, you are shy just seeing yourself in front of a mirror. With the help of NLP, you can channel that identity and become the kind of Man that you want to be.

Beliefs and Values: these are one's personal beliefs and issues that matter to an individual. Believes are fundamental assumptions we have about the world, and, as a result, our values stem from those beliefs. Values are basically what we see as important, and this could include concepts like equality, honesty, education, effort, perseverance, loyalty, and so on. However, not all Men think similarly and there would be different beliefs and values. In a situation where two co-workers with different beliefs and values meet, it is necessary they get along with each other to prevent these differences from affecting their productivity. Some Men find it very difficult to accommodate others who don't share their beliefs and values, and this could affect the company in the long run. One of the best solutions that can help Men get along with others is NLP. It trains the mind in how to accommodate others into our belief and value space.

Capabilities and skills: These are individuals' abilities and what they can do or achieve. There are inner skills and capabilities present in all Men, and they need to be expressed in order to be successful. Some Men believe they have the skill to partake in an exercise or sport; however, due to one reason or the other, they can not fully express themselves. There are thousands of people who have benefited from neuro-linguistic programming, and they have been able to achieve success in their dream profession.

Behaviors: these are specific activities that one performs. There are specific disciplines that need specific sets of behavior for you to be really successful. Behaviors are like our second skin, and they are difficult to put off. Also, change is sometimes hard and can come with a lot of pain and discomfort. As a result, most Men abandon attempts to change bad behavior. In this situation, NLP would be of great help; it helps you seamlessly change from one behavior to another.

Environment: what is referred to as environment is one's context or setting, and this includes people that surround an individual. This is seen as the lowest level of change. Context or settings here could mean home, offices, relaxation spots, and many other things. The truth is the environment has the capacity to affect a Man psychologically. As a result, Men have different perspectives about people and life; sometimes this could be detrimental to them. The truth is that most Men find it difficult to escape from their environment because this is where they were made; they are the product of their upbringing. Men who are from a toxic family or neighborhood find it difficult to relate with people outside those environments, and this could limit their opportunities. With Neuro-linguistic programming, many Men have been able to escape that environmental trauma and live a happy life.

The aim of each level is to arrange and direct the information below it. As a result, therefore, making a change in lower levels can cause changes in the higher level. Also, a change in the higher level can cause changes to the lower levels, as theorized by NLP.

The Benefits Of Neuro-linguistic Programming

You might be thinking this is all very interesting, but how is NLP beneficial to Men, especially Alpha Males? There are numerous positives concerning NLP, and some areas where NLP is beneficial will be highlighted.

Clarity of Vision, Purpose, and Values

Most times, personal development tools and courses are primarily focused on how goals can be set successfully. NLP assists Men to be more aware of the subconscious patterns they express in language and through their senses, and it makes changes to these patterns when necessary.

Neuro-linguistic programming educates Men on how they can involve these in setting their goals and purpose. It also makes them conscious of their current values that inspire their behavior and how to shift them towards a way of life that is energetic.

Overcoming limiting beliefs

Every individual has beliefs that help us. However, there are a few that get in the way of what we want to achieve, and it can be frustrating. In this situation, NLP helps you to reconstruct your current beliefs by infusing various meanings to behaviors and situations in life, and it also develops new beliefs that one would be happy to have. NLP can create a very significant change in a Man's perspective about how they view the world and how they combat the problems of life.

Improved self-confidence

With NLP, there is the possibility of accessing resources from an individual's past or developing new resources for the present and the future. As a result, it can increase the self-confidence of Men in areas where they need it the most. Also, it can educate Men on how they can program themselves to become competent through their unconscious minds.

Managing difficult people

It's very interesting to know that NLP can teach you how to manage people that are difficult. It can teach you how to have productive relationships with people you'd normally have issues with. With NLP, we are able to get along with people we find awkward, or we can make them get along with us. What NLP teaches is the process of building a good means of communication through mirroring and matching at different levels, showing how you can relate with difficult people and assist them in cooperating with you.

Strengthening leadership capabilities

Alpha Males should be able to show leadership qualities. When it comes to developing your leadership capabilities, NLP can be of help. This can include asking questions that are of help at the right time.

Development of new strategies for solving problems

If you want to be successful as an Alpha Male, you should not be too rigid; you want to be open to changes. This course will help you reflect on your current way of thinking and help you develop the ability to think differently. NLP involves examining the way we structure our thoughts unconsciously and how we are able to demystify large chunks of problems, including the ability to reframe problems and convert them into positive situations.

Dealing with pain and allergies

Neuro-linguistics can be used by Men to understand the signals of their bodies and help them to cope with pain. Although you cannot use NLP in all situations, it can help heal allergies developed due to a reaction by the immune system in applicable situations. These allergies can be healed during the period of lower resistance with tools that distance you from the allergy, and you will be able to program yourself back to your healthy state.

Establishing more freedom & choice over our mindset

The mindset of a Man has a huge effect on the kind of person he will be. Alpha Males must know the impact of their mindset in achieving goals and all-round productivity. Whenever we refer to mindset, it includes emotions, performance states, and, most importantly, results. NLP can assist Men when it comes to the development of states, and increasing your performance by the changes of state.

Breaking behavioral patterns

With the mixture of metaphors, intention discovery and motivation, task and training, NLP has the capacity to eradicate unproductive behavioral patterns in Men.

Through a series of NLP interventions that work in the unconscious such as, timeline, N-step reframe, parts integration, and performance coaching, you will have the ability to break poor patterns.

Developing better relationships

Alpha Males should be able to maintain relationships. As an individual, if you want to improve your communication in relationships, NLP can help through the unconscious mind and body.

Improving your coaching skills

With NLP, you are able to learn new methods for how to motivate others and get to the core of complex issues quickly to communicate effectively.

Handling unexpected situations in life

Neuro-linguistic programming can teach you to become resilient to change. Transiting to a certain state will become easier. NLP presents you with a quality method of attaining different perspectives and feelings about changes in your life. NLP can make it easier for Men to deal with people, situations, and emotions in a better way.

Having a good understanding of the capabilities, strategies, and thinking of those that are successful

You will be taught the methods that those that have been successful have used to achieve excellence in their business and life. This can be demonstrated to you via a process known as "Modelling."

Creation of extra energy and relaxation in your life

Going through NLP training, you will discover methods to reduce stress and tiredness, and you will be able to analyze your lifestyle in a clearer way. This will include exercises like breathing and awareness of the senses. You can use these techniques to change your mental state.

Improvement in the team and organizational performance

You will be presented with tools that help you in leading or managing teams through a mixture of perceptual positions and presenting positive states. It presents an effective method of improving your team performance.

Achieving unprecedented success in negotiating and sales

It's no news that we are in a world filled with challenges. As a result, successful tools during negotiation and sales are important. NLP helps you develop better negotiation skills by presenting to you the method of integrating different parts for a better successful result. This is partly due to methods such as having a higher positive intention.

Neuro-linguistic Programming In Therapy

A core concept of NLP is summarized in the saying, "The map is not the territory." This means there are differences between belief and reality. It shows that each Man operates within the context of their perspective, not from the angle of objectivity. Advocates of NLP are of the opinion that everyone's perception of the world is different, distorted, unique, and limited. An individual map of the world is established through data received by the senses. The information acquired can be auditory, visual, olfactory, gustatory, or kinesthetic. It is believed that this information differentiates individuals in terms of quality and importance and that each person processes experience through a primary representational system (PRS).

Concerns And Limitations Of Neuro-linguistic Programming

The major significant question mark about NLP is certainly the lack of verifiable evidence to support the numerous claims made by its proponents. There have been numerous testimonials that have praised the approach. Also, there have been a few scientific studies that provide firm, unbiased proof that it is an effective method of improving one's mentality. The co-founder of NLP, Richard Bandler, has always voiced his discontent with the scientific testing of Neuro-linguistic programming.

However, there are some skeptics. The absence of regulation in training and certification has made many people become NLP practitioners despite them lacking credible experience or a background in mental healthcare.

The application of NLP into everyday life can help Men achieve better results when it comes to decision-making and self-awareness.

As an individual, you would want to create loyalty in your team, and NLP is a major tool that can help you build personal and organizational values. There is a model in NLP called the Neurological or Logical Level of change that is a system for organizational and personal change. This model has proved to us how organizations can work smoothly with their employees to develop better motivation and morale by tying the company values to staff in the workforce.

As a boss, it is better to create a good working relationship with your staff. Studies have shown that most organizational staff leave their position because they feel they are not valued by their superiors. The process of NLP ensures that you are able to work with your staff to enable them to see how valued their post is in the organizational setup. It enables you to show them that the company reflects their own personal values structure. NLP is a process that is effective and one that has been verified by executive coaching subjects. NLP is not restricted to a certain level in the organizational level. It is applicable to all levels.

7

HOW TO FULLY ANALYZE AND INFLUENCE PEOPLE

WE ARE NOW at the fifth Law of Power, which is how to analyze and influence people around us. Either as an entrepreneur or a leader, knowing how to analyze and influence the people around you is vital. Alpha Males are often leaders; this makes it very important for all Alpha Males to understand this power. You must be able to read people's attitudes or countenance to understand what state of mind they are in. As a leader, everything you do rests on your ability to connect with others and work out purposeful relationships. Buying and selling a house, advancing in your careers, selling a product, pitching a story, teaching a course, etc., wouldn't be successful without building a healthy relationship. When you come across a successful manager, their feat isn't brute force, but due to careful appeals that align with their sensibilities. For instance, as a manager, you can't force your workers to do overtime by brute force; yes, they may comply with the added responsibility, but at what expense? If they comply after they have been forced or threatened, be assured that you are losing your relationship with each worker. There are better means of getting people to do what they wouldn't do willingly with a smile on their face, and the best approach is through appeal.

Utilizing these tactics, you can, through a positive influence on others, direct others toward excellence, productivity, and success. As a result, the world has been impacted initially by one person, but the positive ripples will spread. When it comes to influencing people, the truth is that it is centered on the humanity of others. There is every chance that there are Men who are experts at making others feel like a star, and positive results can be achieved as a result of the compliment received. In this situation, the request of others might sound like an atomic bomb to their hearing, but when they're asked by Men who are experts at making someone feel good before requesting anything from them, the request sounds like music to their hearing. They're willing to do what they are instructed to do. Requesting two extra hours from a chef who is changing the shift by four pm will take something special. You can do this by praising the chef's work. Your dishes have been extraordinary, and our kitchen or eatery have been receiving heartfelt compliments from our customers, and this is due to your extraordinary work for our firm. We would like it if you can spare us two of your hours today after your due time. It will be really appreciated by us; our customer needs your service this evening; they've especially asked for you because they've been here before and they adore your dishes.

Or a less effective approach would be - Our customers will be needing your service this evening. You will have to spare two of your hours for us.

These two requests are entirely different, and the former has the tendency to influence the chef more than the latter. It would likely make the chef not only listen but also agree to the request. The relationship between the manager and the chef has not suffered.

How to Analyze People

The better you are at reading an individual, the better you will be able to deal with them; when you are able to understand how another person feels, you can adapt whatever message and communication style to make sure the receiver gets the message in the best possible way.

As regards reading others, there are things Alpha Males should be looking out for, such as signs that can give you a tip-off to what another person is feeling or thinking. These signs would help you to analyze people successfully. As LaRae puts it, "You don't need to be an expert interrogator to figure out what someone else is thinking in their head. The signs and signals are always there for all to see vividly; all it takes is knowing what to look for." Below are nine tips that can be used by Men to read people:

Create a baseline

The fact that people are different means that we all have diverse quirks and patterns of behavior. For instance, someone might clear their throat, stare at the floor while talking, cross their arms during discussions, scratch their head, squint, pout, or jiggle their feet. At first, we might not notice when others are doing these things. If it is the case that we do, we don't pay attention to them. For different reasons, people display these behaviors. They are likely to be mannerisms. However, sometimes, these actions could be pointing to deception, anger, or nervousness. Developing a mental baseline of other people's normal behavior will help Alpha Males in analyzing others.

Look for deviations

It is imperative you pay close attention to inconsistencies between the baseline you have created and the person's gesture and utterances. For example, you have detected that an important goods supplier of yours has the habit of clearing his throat repeatedly when nervous. Whenever he starts to introduce some relatively small changes to your business arrangements, he starts clearing his throat. There is every possibility that there is more here than meets the eye. You can decide to probe further, asking a few questions more than you would have done normally.

Notice clusters of gestures

You should not be in haste to jump to a conclusion during analysis. A lone gesture or word doesn't necessarily mean anything; however, when several behavioral aberrations are clumped together, you must take note. It might be the case that your staff member doesn't only clear his throat while speaking to you; they might also be scratching their head and shuffling their feet. Success in analyzing people would require Alpha Males to proceed with caution and remain confident in their abilities.

Compare and contrast

Fine, you might have noticed that someone is acting up a little differently than normal. You should up your observation a bit and see if and when such a person repeats the same behavior alongside others in your group. You should continually observe the person as he or she communicates with others in the room. Take note of the changes in the person's expression; pay attention to such a person's posture and body language.

Look in the mirror

Mirror neurons are built-in monitors that exist in our brain that display other people's states of mind. We are wired when it comes to reading one another's body language. Whenever we smile, it activates the smile muscle in our faces, while frown activities also activate our frown muscles. Our eyebrows arch, facial muscles relax, blood flows to our lips, making them full when we see someone we admire. If your partner doesn't return that behavior, the person could be transmitting a clear message to you; it could be the case that he or she doesn't like you as much as you like them, or they aren't happy with something you have done.

Identify the strong voice

It doesn't always happen that the most powerful person is the one sitting at the head of the table. One major indicator of strong Men is that they have strong voices. It could happen that in a conference room, the most confident person is most likely to be the person with the ultimate power: they are characterized by expansive posture, strong voice, and a big smile. A loud voice must not be confused with a strong voice. If you are at the helm of pitching an idea to a group, it's easy to pay close attention to the leader of the team. But there is every possibility that the leader has a weak personality. In fact, such a person relies on others to make decisions, and that person is usually easily influenced. If you are able to recognize the strong voice, your chances of success will increase dramatically.

Pay attention to the way they talk

Most times, Men who shuffle along lack a free movement in their motion. Keeping your head down can denote a lack of self-confidence. Whenever you notice something like this in your group, you should make the extra effort to offer commendation to help build the person's confidence. In other cases, you can ask such a person some direct questions during a meeting just to reach those great ideas that may be hidden inside them.

Pinpoint action words

Ask any FBI agent the best way to get into someone's head; their answers would be through words. Words represent thoughts, so it is important we identify words that are laden with meaning. For instance, if your boss uses the word "decided," this means that your boss is not impulsive, has weighed different options, and has thought things through. Action words offer insights into the way others think.

Pay attention to personality clues

We are all from different backgrounds, and, as a result, we have our unique traits, but there are basic clarifications that can help your relationships with other people so you can read them accurately. How does he or she handle risk and uncertainty? What inflates their ego? What behavior traits do they depict when they are relaxed?

Now that we have known how to analyze others, it is important we put this into perspective and move a step further and influence them positively. Below are some important tips that show how Alpha Males can have a positive influence on others.

Be authentic

If you want to have a positive influence on others, it is imperative that you are authentic. You shouldn't be a reflection of someone else's character or version of authenticity. Unmask what it is that makes you special so as to start making a positive impact on others.

You should make a unique decision on an issue and then live up to and honor that decision you have made. Social media influencers have a great deal of influence on others because they have created a niche for themselves. Or it may be they've encountered a common issue, and they approached that issue from a new or novel way. It is no secret that people appreciate those whose public persona tallies with their persona in private. The fact is that most people crave stability, we get bothered anytime we encounter contradictions. If people claim to be one way, but they act contrary to that image, then we tend to see them as confused, untrustworthy, and not authentic. All these combinations do not bode well for positive influence on others.

Listen

The best advice my dad gave me when I was growing up is that I should listen carefully when others speak. He said if I can become a good listener, I will know all that is needed to be known as regards a person's point of view, character, desire, and needs.

As a Man who craves power, it is vital you learn how to influence people; therefore, you should be an expert in listening to what is said and what is left unsaid. In this lies the explanation for what people need to feel validated and supported. If a person feels they are invisible and obscure to their leaders, there is every possibility that they wouldn't be influenced positively by that person. When you are able to listen genuinely to a person and identify their major need for validation and acceptance, it builds positive energy in them.

Become an Expert

Generally, people are predisposed to listen to, if not respect, higher authority. If you want to have a positive influence on others, become an authority in the field where you will like to motivate others. Take that extra step to read and research everything you can as regards a given topic, then take a step further by looking for opportunities that will help you put your education into practice. When it comes to arguing, it is best done over opinions rather than facts, and experts come with facts.

Lead with a story

Having worked in public relations, I came to understand that personal narratives, testimonials, and impact stories are powerful tools. However, I am always amazed at how effective a well-timed and well-narrated story can be. If you want to have a positive influence on others, you should educate yourself on how to tell stories. However, your stories should have a connection to the issue or concept you are discussing. You should always present an analogy or metaphor that explains the topic you are discussing in simple terms and in clear detail. A story told in the right way has the tendency to capture the attention and emotions of your listener. Learning how to tell a story will help you learn how to influence other people positively.

Lead by example

This subtopic is almost a cliché. There is nothing more inspiring than watching passionate, talented people working or playing; they just give a different vibe. One of the reasons a person who isn't a fanatic of a certain profession can be in awe of a profession they aren't interested in is because human nature appreciates the extraordinary. When we see the Olympics, gymnastic competitions, and other competitive sports, we can easily recognize the effort of people who are passionate and give their all whenever they are competing. As humans, we all want to celebrate the extraordinary accomplishments and believe that the example they have set is proof that we too can accomplish something great; it doesn't have to be qualifying for the Olympics. It is important that you lead in a positive way if you want to influence people to do well. You should lead by example, with good intentions, and make sure you execute with aplomb.

Catch people doing good

A powerful tool that can be used in influencing others is to get them into the habit of doing good. Rather than looking for problems, look for successes. You should be in search of things that are critically important to your peers and subordinates, things that managers have done to make work more effective and enjoyable but have been overlooked. Once you can get people into the mindset of doing good, you should name and acknowledge their contributions. Make sure your countenance shows you are interested in others' success, as this surely impacts all the personal relationships you set out to create positively. To have an impact on others' lives is as easy as giving them a compliment for a job well done.

Be effusive with praise

It was easy for me to quickly notice a remarkable trait of one of my former bosses. In all of his meetings, he makes sure he starts them with praises and ends them with praises. However, he peppered praise all through the meeting. He will always find a way to celebrate the unique attributes and skills of his team members. He doesn't lack the ability to quickly and concisely assess what others were doing well, and he would always let their colleagues be aware of their contribution.

Meetings shouldn't always be an occasion to go through a "to-do" list; they should be an avenue to celebrate others' accomplishments regardless of how little they are. This is very useful when learning how to influence others.

This inevitably has a positive influence on the people you're surrounded with. Always know that when people feel appreciated, they will be willing to go above and beyond whenever you request anything from them.

Be kind

There is every chance that you can easily get entangled in a cycle of proving yourself. We all love to be right; it's a basic human trait. But be careful about letting it cloud your judgment. Being right all the time is important for people who lack confidence or, strangely enough, who place the opinion of others above theirs. One's ego is fed when one is perceived as being right. However, it should be noted that in your quest to be right, you can hurt other people and build resentment. Once someone is hurt by you being unkind, it's very hard to make them listen to what you are trying to influence them to do; the damage has been done. The solution to dealing with people through bullying is to place kindness above rightness. Many people are of the opinion that they need other people to validate their experience. You shouldn't get offended when people do not perceive the situation you experienced the same way you do; your experience is personal to you, not others. You and your friends could go out to have dinner, and you got food poisoning; you do not need the validation of your friends that the food served at dinner was problematic for you.

All the validation you need is your own experience of food poisoning. Therefore, trying to be right is essentially wasting time; in a situation where you became unkind to your friends while seeking validation for your food poisoning experience, you have really lost points.

Understand people's needs: logical, emotional, and cooperative

It has been argued by the Center for Creative Leadership that the best method to influence people is to appeal to their logical, emotional, and cooperative needs. Their logical needs relate to their rational and educational needs. Their emotional need is the information that appeals to their personal manner. At the same time, the cooperative need is understanding various levels of cooperation, and accurately offering them. The key to this system is that you have to understand that different people need different things. For some, emotional appeals influence them more than logical explanations. For others, they elevate the chance to exchange ideas with others over the emotional connection. You must know your subordinates in order to know what they need to be positively influenced. Having only a little information about the audience you are attempting to influence will be ineffective.

Understand your lane

To effectively influence other people, learn how to operate from your sphere of influence, your place of expertise. Every other thing should be left to others. The world has moved on from the era when a jack-of-all-trades was celebrated. Brands that under- stand their target audience and can supply a specific need are appreciated. You should focus on what you are uniquely gifted and qualified to do, and you should offer the gift to the people who are in need of it. This way, you are more effective. This effectiveness becomes attractive. Being occupied with what others do well, rather than what you do well, is a habit that will limit your positive influence on others.

Centering your humanity is the best method to learn how to influence people. If you want to make use of positive influence, pay attention to the way you communicate, and, initially, improve the relationship with yourself. When you've done that, you can relate to others. It is very hard to influence others if you are still in the process of figuring out how you should communicate with yourself. You should get comfortable with your uniqueness first before going out to influence others.

8

HYPNOSIS TECHNIQUES

IF YOU HAVE BEEN READING from the beginning, you should have seen the kind of emphasis I have placed on the mind. The human mind is very powerful, and it is the source of absolute power. You might have seen the power of Hypnosis on screen in several movies; famous examples are *Get out* and *Captain*

America. One thing is common in these movies, the person hypnotized loses control of their bodies to the hypnotist. Many believe it is unrealistic and cannot be used in the real world, but it can. You just have to know how it is done.

What is Hypnosis?

Hypnosis is simply a natural state that grants access directly to the subconscious mind, the part that houses the learned behavior pattern-making systems. In layman's terms, what it means is that your types of decisions, reactions, and behaviors are stored in a portion of the mind. You might have noticed that you can do some things without overthinking. These actions are kept in the subconscious mind, and the use of Hypnosis can trigger them.

If you are getting hypnotized, you will be in a trance-like mental state where your attention and concentration are increased. In this state, it is easy for people to suggest things to you. The hypnotic state has often been described as being in a sleep-like state but with an increased level of attention. When you are in this state, you will likely feel sleepy and zoned-out, but you are aware and sensitive to suggestions.

There have been many false ideas about Hypnosis; most of them were generated from what people see in movies. However, contrary to what many believe, Hypnosis is a natural process, and it can even be used as a therapeutic tool. The effectiveness of Hypnosis depends on the subconscious mind.

The power of the subconscious mind

Before I start explaining the subconscious mind, let us first determine what consciousness even means. Consciousness simply means being aware of things around and in your mind. There is no perfect definition of what consciousness means since there are different levels of consciousness. However, it is safe to say that an average person spends most of their day on conscious activities like bathing, eating, going to work, hanging out with friends, families, and loved ones. All of them should be done while you are awake, except, a few times, in dreams.

However, we are not always in the normal state of consciousness, and sometimes deviations occur. An altered state of functioning occurs when you experience a change in the quality of your mental functioning pattern. The hypnosis state is similar to full consciousness, but with some exceptions. In the hypnosis state, the subject is entirely focused, and they are relatively unbothered with typical distractions of reasoning. Your muscles will also be relaxed, and there is an increase in the sensitivity of the senses.

Since Hypnosis can even be called a natural state, the subject will not go into an unending trance if a hypnotist stops the Hypnosis abruptly. However, the response differs. Some subjects would be extremely surprised by the disappearance of the hypnotist, and they'd want to return to normal consciousness. Some could also just start sleeping, and they'd wake up naturally after their sleep. Most times in Hypnosis, the control lies with the subject, and the hypnotist cannot do things against the subject's will.

How to use Hypnosis?

If you want to be able to use Hypnosis, you must understand how Hypnosis can serve you. You should know that it is essential that you stop and question the reason for hypnotizing someone and the motivation behind it. There are many reasons why Men want to harness the power of Hypnosis. Some guys want to know more because they want to learn practical hypnotic techniques for themselves and the people around them. It could also be because you want to learn some skills for your job while some like me just want to increase their influence.

No matter the reasons for learning Hypnosis, the same techniques apply. All you have to know is how. You should know that Hypnosis is not mind control, and you can do it without manipulating the other party to do your bidding. This power can be used by all Men. How a Man can use it is explained below.

How to hypnotize someone?

There are many methods written in books, journals, etc., about Hypnosis. It's not as complicated as many make it out to be; two main steps are popularly used. The first step of Hypnosis is called hypnotic induction, where the hypnotist will put the subject in a state where they are more open to suggestions. This is called a trance, and there are many techniques for induction. They are;

Relaxation technique

Some of you might have visited a therapist and must have heard words like, "Make yourself comfortable." You might have even wondered why the environment is so roomy; some even provide their subjects with couches to lie down on. This is one of the techniques used in Hypnosis because the subject is more likely to fall into a trance when they are relaxed. The trance is the first goal in Hypnosis, and it makes the subject more open to indirect suggestions. There are some popular methods of relaxation such as:

- Controlled breathing
- Speak in a soft tone
- Lie down

- Relax and tense muscles
- Counting down in your head
- Make yourself comfortable

Handshake technique

This was famously used by a Man popularly regarded as the father of hypnotherapy; his name was Milton Erickson. He used the handshake technique to induce a hypnotic trance. The most common form of greeting in modern society is with handshakes, but this greeting can also be used to shock the subconscious by disruption. This technique is used by professional hypnotists as they disrupt the conventional societal norm by pulling the subject forward and off-balance. This sudden and unexpected disruption makes the mind open to suggestions.

Visualization

Visualization can be used to make suggestions and induce trances. You can ask your subjects to recollect arrangements in a room that is familiar to them. For example, the paintings, the smell, light, and window shape. You should then move on to a room less familiar to them, and as they struggle to recall the information about that room, their minds will be open to suggestions. You can use this technique to remember positive memories and associate them with a reward. You can also use it to change someone's view about a negative image.

Eye cues

The brain has two spheres for reasoning. The right sphere is responsible for conscious and creative thoughts, while the left deals with practical ideas and the subconscious. When you are having a conversation with someone, you can check for feedback from the listener by studying their reactions. You can look at the listener's eyes to determine what part of the brain they are using to react to your statements. Check if they are looking to the right to use the conscious side or the left for the subconscious. If your listener is looking at the left, you can make suggestions that they will not be consciously aware of.

Arm "levitation" Technique

This was also used by the father of Hypnosis, and it is a classic Ericksonian technique. This starts with the subject closing their eyes and is followed by noticing differences in feelings in the arms. The hypnotherapist should make suggestions about the sensations the subject is feeling in each arm. Feelings in these arms could range from heavy to light, hot to cold. After this, the subject will enter a trance and could lift their arm physically, or they might believe they have raised their arms without any actual movement. If you see any of the above, the induction was successful.

Sudden shock or falling backward

This is similar to the handshake technique, and here the subject is shocked into a trance. You should do this cautiously, and I would also advise that you do not risk causing any physical pain to your subject. Some Men use trust falls to shock the subconscious into a trance if they are strong enough to carry the subject. The sensation that is experienced from falling backward shocks the system and leaves the mind open to suggestions. This technique is not advisable for all Men and you only should use this technique if you are sure that you will not drop the subject.

Eye fixation

Many times during this book, I have emphasized that it is important that Alpha Males remain focused. And focus can be used for hypnotism. Have you ever zoned out when you were staring at something interesting in a room while someone is talking? If yes, did you miss their whole speech and could not recollect anything that was said? This means that you have been in a trance. Focusing on an object can be used to induce trance. Famous examples include a swinging pocket watch and a pendulum. These are commonly used in stage hypnosis, and although they can be used, their popularity will make you encounter more resistance and likely fail. If you want to use this technique, you just need to understand the secrets behind eye fixation. There are two secrets; the first is that the object occupies the conscious mind, which opens the subconscious mind to suggestion. The second is that moving the eyes back and forth is energy-demanding for the eye, and the eyes become physically tired.

Bodyscan

This is commonly used for self-hypnosis. You should start by scanning your body from head to feet with your eyes closed. You should start from the top of the body. Notice all sensations in the body, including the beard on your face, the expansion of your ribcage with your breath, each finger extension, the feeling of the chair on your buttocks. You can work from either direction, but cover everything from the top of your head to your feet. Repeat this process until you enter into a trace.

Countdown breathing

You could have heard that while people meditate, it is essential to control their breathing, but this is also applicable in self-hypnosis. Here is a brief illustration of how it works:

- Sit upright in a chair, put your arms on your lap and close your eyes.
- Breathe in deeply through your nose and release the air from your mouth.
- With slow controlled breaths, start the count down from 100.
- Each release of air counts as one interval.
- After you are done, you should be in a trance, but if you are not, repeat the exercise and count down from a higher number.

After you have induced the subject by Hypnosis, you should start introducing the suggestions that you want. Suggestions are the reason why Hypnosis is carried out; it is the desired behavior that the subject wants. The suggestions that you introduce when the subject is in a trance are called hypnotic suggestions. We have two main schools of thought for suggestions.

Indirect suggestion

The indirect suggestion is highly used and favored by hypnotherapists. You can use it because control is given to the subject. The indirect suggestion respects the subject's boundaries and does not deviate from clinical ethics. Studies have also shown that this form of suggestion is more effective in subjects that are resistant or are unsure about trances. Here, you do not need to order the subject, and it goes more like a request. For example, "You can close your eyes when you are comfortable."

Direct suggestion

Direct suggestion is sometimes viewed as unethical because the subject is powerless to the suggestions of the hypnotherapist. Here the power of Hypnosis lies exclusively with the hypnotist, and the subject is defenseless and helpless to stop the behavioral changes. What you have to do here is give an explicit command that the subject must perform. It is often used to correct behaviors. For example, it has been used in the Stanford Prison experiment to exercise authority and instill obedience by manipulating the subjects. Examples of popular direct suggestions are;

- Close your eyes.
- You will now go to sleep.
- You will now listen to everything I say.
- You will quit smoking.

Hypnotic trigger

We have many forms of hypnotic triggers, and we can have more. The form of trigger used depends on the hypnotherapist. Since you are the one using it, the trigger will be anything you choose. You can use the trigger to remind the subconscious of the subject of a desired reaction or feeling that was suggested under Hypnosis. Examples include:

- snap of fingers
- bell sounds
- opening a door
- standing or sitting down

Misdirection

Misdirection is an advanced hypnotherapy technique that is often used in the real world. Just as the name implies, it involves deceiving the audience by leading them in the wrong direction. You might have observed the use of this technique in various fields such as sports, entertainment, and politics. We have two types of misdirection which are mental misdirection and literal misdirection. A typical example of the use of misdirection can be seen in magic shows. Most magic tricks work with misdirection; for example, a magician could be waving a hand on one side while performing a sleight of hand on the other. The magician guides the audience to where he wants them to look and sneaks a card up his sleeve making them think the card disappeared. In Hypnosis, misdirection can be a visualization. You can hypnotize a subject who's dealing with anxiety by using misdirection to make them believe that they are relaxed on a beach whenever they feel worried. This directs them away from an unpleasant image.

Hypnosis in 5 steps

Although there are techniques that you can use, Alpha Males can also learn how to hypnotize someone with five simple steps. These steps will be explained below:

. . .

Establishing a relationship

By now, every Man reading this book should understand the possibilities in relationships, and once again, it is important to consider them. The first thing you should do if you want to hypnotize someone is to build a good relationship. You might have heard the ritual sayings popularly used in hypnotherapy circles. If you're going to use a script to hypnotize someone, this part will provide you with important information about the person's background. This will also help you create a rapport with the person that will increase the efficiency of Hypnosis. You can do this by asking questions.

You need to establish some sort of relationship, preferably a good one, if you want to hypnotize someone. Contrary to popular movies, hypnotism is not about waving a vintage pocket watch in someone's face and expecting them to become your subjects. When you want to hypnotize someone, it is essential that you understand the kind of words that they use so that you can incorporate them into your Hypnosis. Just as Hypnosis can be used for personal benefit, it can also be beneficial to the person hypnotized. For example, if you want to use it at work with a coworker or boss, you can meet them for drinks without being inappropriate. The purpose of this is to meet them at a location where they can be themselves, and it is easy to know more about them. The change of scenery can help you be more comfortable with yourself. If you are sure they can be comfortable with you at work, you can also do it there. This step will help you in the next stage that is called the hypnotic induction.

Hypnotic induction and deepeners

Hypnotic induction and deepeners

As I have mentioned earlier and will probably mention again, Hypnosis is not complicated and all Men can do it. All you have to do is get the person into an increased state of focus and concentration, removing all distractions that could take over the mind. What you have to do in this stage is ensure that you have the person's full attention, which you will achieve by introducing a trance. You can practice hypnosis in many ways. Since many do not believe that Hypnosis is real, you can even tell them if they would like to try Hypnosis. This is a means of asking permission.

There are some techniques that you can use, but here I will be explaining rapid transformation therapy. This therapy is an improvement on traditional approaches that used to take a lot of time. You can use a rapid eye movement technique that will help you achieve your goals faster. This technique is also simple to understand. In this technique, what you have to do is tell the person to roll their eyes while closing it for some moments. After the eyes are closed, you should notice the flickering of their eyes under the eyelids.

These movements help the person relax and assist them in getting into a trance state. Once you are able to get them into a trance state, the next thing will be how to deepen the state. There are much deeper hypnotic inductions that you can use. When you want to hypnotize, you should have more than one at hand if the first method is not effective. It should be a selection of deeper inductions that could work. You can do this by repeating relaxing phrases such as, "The sounds you hear now will cause you to go deeper into a soothing relaxation, and you are going deeper into a calm state of relaxation." The effectiveness of what you say depends on the tone that is used to say these things. If you are using a script, ensure that you read this part with a smooth and melodic voice. The tone makes it easy for the person to relax.

The goal here is relaxation, and you should try all means to ensure that they are relaxed. This process should not be rushed. It starts from the tone, which is followed by speaking gently. Your voice should be rhythmic and have cadence if you want to induce someone into a deep hypnotic state. Sometimes you might not need a deeper state before the person is fully relaxed, but a deepener will always come in handy if the person is not relaxed. The function of the deepener is in the name as it deepens the relaxation. If you do it well, the person should slowly relax until they reach a point where they are totally relaxed.

You should know the signs that show when the person you are using this technique is in a trance. There are many signs, and you might not be able to see all of them. However, you should ensure that you are looking for some of these cues in your subjects:

- Lip licking
- Flickering movements of the eyes
- Slight jerks of legs, hands, and feet
- Reduced swallowed movements
- Changes in the rhythm of breathing
- Uncontrolled micro-movements of the lips and body
- Shoulders slumping and head drooping
- Changes in skin color of the face
- Rapid Eye Movement under the eyelids
- Crying

Some of the signs that denote change are very subtle, and you have to be aware of them. Sometimes people that have been hypnotized are unaware of what is really happening. The reactions of subjects to hypnosis techniques are different, and there are no rules that regulate the behaviors.

Hypnotic imagery

This stage will test the skill of your hypnotic techniques as it focuses on the main reason why you are hypnotizing someone. In this stage, you can choose to use hypnotic metaphors or imagery. Any Man that wants to be successful with this skill must know how to make use of his mind. One of the ways that you can do that is by using the part of the mind that deals with imagination. The imagination of humans is a potent weapon, and this part plays a massive role in Hypnosis. The aim of this stage is to use hypnotic imagery and metaphors to excite the imagination of your subjects.

If you want to use Hypnosis, you must be able to stimulate the subconscious mind of your subjects and expose limiting beliefs and unconscious blocks, if there are any. This stage is also known as the suggestion phase, and the things you will say depends on the goal of the Hypnosis. If you want your boss to grant you leave or a raise, you can tell a story about another employee that did something similar which had a good ending for the boss. In this stage, you could offer some suggestions about how the act would benefit him or her. If you want your partner to be more confident, you can give some essential suggestions like you have inner confidence or your persona exudes confidence. You could also say that the subject is a very beautiful and confident person.

You can use hypnotic imagery to create suggestions in the mind of your subjects. In this stage of Hypnosis, you rid the subject of blocks in their subconscious mind. The scripts that are used to form the story used in hypnotic imagery are often similar in many ways. If you want Hypnosis to be effective, you have to deliver the news like it is a sales pitch. Studies have shown that repetition is the best way for the mind to learn because it can strengthen the neural pathway. What you will do is that you will repeat what you have said again and again to ensure it is retained by the mind.

Future state

Once you have introduced a suggestion into the mind of the subject, you can now proceed to the desired future state that you are trying to achieve. At this stage, you will be able to make your subject imagine or picture what you want them to see or do. In this stage, you allow your subject to visualize the impact of their decision. Here they will see the end result and how the decisions impacted their lifestyles some months after making the desired changes. For example, if you want your partner to lose some weight after you have hypnotized her, you can create a future where she is your desired size and shape. It could also be about their attitude towards life, including your relationship; then, you can show her how happy she would be if her attitude changed. When you help them envision the future that you want, it helps to change their mindset to visualize success. This also allows the subconscious mind to work towards the desired goal.

Embed the suggestions

The suggestions that you want your subjects to reflect must be embedded into the mind. You can do this in many ways by repeating the positive suggestion, such as, "Your mind is clear and focused on a goal," depending on what the goal is. After declaring the suggestions, you can now say that, "The suggestions are permanently embedded into your subconscious mind." You can also increase the efficiency of the power of the subconscious mind by saying that the thought will grow stronger in your mind over the following days and weeks. You can embed your suggestions before the final stage, and it will still be effective.

After you have completed the stages of Hypnosis on someone, you can now bring them back into their reality. You should do this slowly and in steps and make sure that you do not bring your subjects into an awake state and their environment too quickly. The first thing is that you should make the person aware of their surroundings by using verbal signs. Ensure that the subject knows that they are about to regain total consciousness. I do this by telling them that I am going to count to seven, and when I count seven, you will regain your consciousness. If you and the subject are willing to discuss their feelings during the session, the feedback will help you become a better hypnotist. You should ask questions like how they felt during the Hypnosis or if they experience a pullback to the awake state that you don't know about.

Benefits of Hypnosis

Similar to most of the laws of power, the outcome of this power depends on who is wielding it. The power of Hypnosis can be beneficial to Men that know how to use it. Some of the benefits that it gives Men are;

It improves relationships

The undeniable social nature of humans is evident as we crave intimacy and connection. Although this makes us stronger, it also makes our relationships affect us deeply, no matter the type of the relationship. Men are not immune to pain and even Alpha Males experience hurt and pain. You might have experienced hurt from are invested in them. Some of the hurt that you might encounter might have come while you were young, and it has affected all your relationships, even as an adult. You can use Hypnosis to understand why you feel the way you do and your behaviors in your relationship. It can also provide support by showing you new ways of thinking. In relationships, it is impossible to avoid conflicts, and it is healthy for you to experience them. Conflicts allow you to see things from different perspectives, but there is a limit. If a conflict has become a constant presence in your relationship and the arguments occur with anger and malice, you should question things. You can solve conflicts by having honest conversations to reveal some hidden resentments. However, you can also correct these feelings by using Hypnosis. I have had my fair share of toxic relationships where it looks like the arguments never end. It always seemed like we were arguing about the same things again and again. I always took this as a sign that the relationship has reached its breaking point, but this is not always true. Such patterns could come as a result of an internal battle occurring in the subconscious mind.

You can use hypnotherapy to get to the source of the conflict and to confirm if it relates to the turmoil in your subconscious mind. This can be done by putting you in a state of Hypnosis where you will be more willing to accept suggestions.

Restore confidence

Another impact of toxic relationships can be damaged confidence. Every Man should be confident, and hypnosis can help Men address issues of confidence. I said that I have been in some unhealthy relationships where my partner derives pleasure in making me feel bad about myself. I am sure this is not an exclusive experience. There are other Men battling something similar. Some guys might have experienced or are in such situations, and some are trying to leave. You should know that there are challenges involved in leaving relationships. Sometimes you might not have the confidence and the self-esteem that you need to leave such a relationship. Leaving the relationship is not the only hard part, as living with the knowledge can also be very difficult. Those memories can affect you as you try to get back to normal. You might have endured some things that could make it hard for you to build up your confidence. You can hypnotize yourself or go to therapies that use some hypnosis techniques to address the patterns that are causing a lasting effect. You can use hypnosis techniques to reconnect with yourself and what you need. The hypnosis techniques will try to tap into the unlimited amount of power that you have within and encourage you to walk with your head held high.

Build confidence

One of the things that I do not enjoy is the realization that I have to start going on dates after a break-up. Opening up and meeting new people brings a kind of vulnerability that is difficult for many. This is often a struggle for many Men, especially in terms of confidence. It is no secret that you have a better chance of having successful dates when you are confident. The lack of confidence and fear of getting hurt might have caused me to build up walls and not let others in. However, instead of building walls, you should try and build up your confidence. Fear and lack of confidence can make dating extremely difficult for you. If you are not confident, it is easy for you to lose sight of the things that you want and deserve. Lack of confidence makes you think that this is the best you can do, even if that is not what you want. However, this lack of confidence can be corrected by the use of hypnosis techniques. You can change negative feelings about yourself, such as I don't deserve love. Hypnosis can help Men locate the source of the loss of confidence and encourage the creation of new behavioral patterns.

Managing anxiety

There will be moments in life where some Men might experience anxiety. Hypnosis works with the brain, and feelings of anxiety originate from the brain based on what you are thinking. You can use Hypnosis to manage these feelings. Sometimes anxiety stems from past trauma, and you can overcome these traumatic memories by Hypnosis.

Achieving goals

Just as Men can use Hypnosis on others, you can also use it to achieve personal goals. Any Man that is able to use this power on others can also channel it into his personal life. Some do this by setting their subconscious mind on a goal that they work towards. If you want to achieve your goals, it must start from the mind. You can make that goal a focus by putting it in your subconscious mind. It will make you focused on your goal and determined to achieve it. It will make you single-minded while working towards your goal.

How to develop the power of Hypnosis

The power of Hypnosis is available for anyone that is ready to work for it. After you have read the techniques and you know what Hypnosis is about, you should know that it can be used by all Men. Here I will show you ways that Men can use to develop this power.

Practice

If you want to be able to use this power when you need it or when you want to, you have to practice it. Hypnosis is a skill like many others, and you will only get better with practice. With practice, you will learn how you can quickly enter into a trace or induce a subject into a trance. Practice will help you increase your portfolio of hypnotic suggestions to improve the outcome of Hypnosis. For example, if you love watching sports, how do you think Stephen Curry is able to make half-court shots regularly? The answer is practice. Although most Men might not be able to make shots from 40 ft, any Man can be a good hypnotist if they practice.

Have a goal in mind

When you want to hypnotize someone or yourself, ensure that there is a goal to be achieved. In a relationship, the goal could be to reduce the anxiety of your partner. Having goals gives you a better chance to have focused and productive sessions.

Schedule time

The most important aspect and often the hardest part is getting started with Hypnosis. You can improve on your techniques for Hypnosis by setting aside some time daily and writing it down in your schedule. You can perform hypnotic techniques at various times of the day or night.

Abuse of the power of Hypnosis

This law of power can also be abused like many others. If the hypnotist decides to harm the subject when they are in a trance, this is obviously completely unjustifiable behavior. Harm in Hypnosis could be giving suggestions that are not beneficial to the life of the subject. During the trance state, your subject is not only open to good suggestions; bad suggestions can also be embedded in the subconscious.

There are also hypnotic triggers that come with hypnotherapy. The triggers of hypnotic behavioral changes should only be given to a select few because they can be abused. When this power is abused, it can severely affect the quality of life of the subject. Alpha Males that want to use this power should ensure they understand the consequences of the power so as to avoid hurting others.

By now, you should know indeed that the power of Hypnosis is something attainable. You can use this chapter as a guide to know what Hypnosis means and its relationship to the subconscious mind. I have also talked about the benefits, usage, and ways that you can use to develop this law of power.

9

EMOTIONAL INTELLIGENCE

HAVE you met Men who always find a way to conduct themselves in an appropriate manner and adjust to awkward situations without losing their composure? You could have wondered how such Men can handle tough and complicated situations with such poise, grace, and elegance. Men who can handle dicey situations in the best way often have high emotional intelligence. Such Men are often Alpha Males.

What Is Emotional Intelligence?

Emotional intelligence is the capability of someone to understand their feelings and those of others. It involves having several skills (emotional and social) that improve how we are perceived because of how we express ourselves. These skills assist you in analyzing and dealing with challenges; it also helps you maintain social relationships by using vital information meaningfully and effectively. Emotional intelligence is affected by emotional self-awareness.

All Men must have emotional intelligence because it has a huge effect on human lives. Emotional intelligence would assist you in identifying what your strengths and weaknesses are and how they will affect other aspects of your life. If you can identify all parts of yourself, including the ones that are tough to accept, it gives you a better chance of understanding your stress factors and the things that make you happy. Emotionally intelligent Men know how to manage their behavioral traits while navigating through challenges to give them the best chances of success in all their relationships.

All human beings feel different kinds of emotions, and sometimes those emotions can get us to make right choices or wrong choices. The ability to manage data about your feelings and the reason why you are behaving in a certain way deals with emotional intelligence. Emotional intelligence assists you to make the right decisions at different points in life. Emotions can help you achieve excellence, but they can also be a trigger for impulsive responses.

There are many roles that emotions play in the lives of Men. Studies have shown that emotional intelligence has an important role in success. There are also some suggestions that emotional intelligence is even more vital than the intelligent quotient of individuals. If you want to be successful and enjoy all the benefits of being an Alpha Male, you must learn the secrets of emotional intelligence. It is easy to identify people who are emotionally intelligent as they are usually the ones at the top of corporate hierarchies, and they know how to manage relationships. I consider myself an example since many people have asked how I have been able to maintain a good relationship with my ex-wives without stepping on the toes of my girlfriend. Although it is not always easy, it became a lot simpler when I harnessed the power of emotional intelligence.

Alpha Males are emotionally intelligent, and this is one of the reasons people want to be around them. Everyone wants to feel good about themselves, and we are drawn to people who have this quality and who can inspire it in others. It is important to work on your emotional intelligence as it can improve with time, unlike the intelligent quotient that remains the same throughout a person's life.

Principles Of Emotional Intelligence

There are many benefits associated with emotional intelligence, which makes it essential for anyone that wants to be an Alpha Male. One of the benefits is that it bestows power to whoever is able to use it. However, if you want to know how to use it, you must know about its principles as well, which will be explained below:

Self-Awareness

Self-awareness is the ability of an individual to identify and understand personal emotions. This is an important skill in emotional intelligence because this ability does not only affect you. Self-awareness extends beyond identifying personal emotions; a Man who is self-aware will be able to recognize the effect of his emotions, moods, and actions on others. For example, after a long day at work where things did not go his way - he could have lost his job, loved one, or something dear to him. The normal human reaction to this could be anger, sadness, and sometimes frustration. When you have such days, it is easy for you to flare up due to the things that you are feeling, but a Man with strong self-awareness will understand how to control his emotions, so he does not appear rude, angry, and cause damage to others. You might be saying grief is difficult to control, and I know that; I have also experienced some loss in my life, but you should also know that during the brief moment where you flare up, your actions can cause irreversible damage.

Any Man that wants to become self-aware must know how to monitor his emotions and understand various emotional reactions. This should be followed by correctly identifying all emotions based on reactions. If you want to be self-aware, you should understand the relationship between your behavior and feelings.

As a human being, it is normal not to know everything or be good at everything; we all have strengths and weaknesses. However, having weaknesses does not make you less of a person as long as you are ready to admit it and work on your weaknesses if it is possible. Men who are self-aware are always aware of their strengths and weaknesses, and this does not stop them from living their normal lives. Men who are self-aware have an open mind towards experiencing new things, learning new information from different sources; it could be from their interactions with others. Such Men are confident, have an excellent sense of humor and know-how. They are respected by people around them. You can identify such individuals with their behaviors as they are kind, respectful, humble, and they always display inclusivity.

Self-regulation

Self-regulation is the ability to keep emotions under control and channel disruptive outbursts and moods away from others. This does not mean that you should hide your emotions and keep them pent-up inside; self-regulation means that instead of expressing emotions and moods through outbursts, you suspend expression and wait until you can express them appropriately. This is not easy as some people can be annoying, especially some bosses at work. It was not easy for me to master this principle, and many times I struggled with it. Growing up, I was always into fights, sometimes verbal and some physical, because I could not control my emotions. Most times, after such occurrences, I would always blame the person that caused me to react, but I soon discovered that it was my own problem. The first step I took to control this problem was that whenever I got angry, I would leave the scene and would not return until I was calm.

Self-regulation means that you will be able to determine how you choose to express your emotions and you don't lose your temper readily in front of others. If you are quick to anger because of the actions of others, it means that you have given them power over you. Alpha Males should be the ones exerting this power and not the other way around. Any Man who is able to control his emotions will rarely make rash and hasty emotional decisions. Such a Man will also have reduced instances where he verbally attacks someone else or gossips. Men with high regulation skills do not compromise what they stand for based on their emotions. When you are able to control your emotions and only express them at the right moments, you will be trusted and respected by the people around you. Such individuals are able to settle tough and difficult situations by good conflict management styles.

Social skills

The social skills that you have are a vital aspect of your emotional intelligence. Alpha Males are often seen as leaders wherever they are, sometimes even without being in any leadership position. They're seen as leaders because of the influence they have. This influence is garnered by their social skills and it will help you to have meaningful relationships with others. Building relationships with people will provide more information about yourself and help you understand others better. The information that you have obtained from your social skills will be useless unless you incorporate it into daily communications. Some might say they prefer to be on their own and do not see the need for social skills, but as long as you are human, you will need someone else for something, no matter how insignificant.

As an Alpha Male, you should have good social skills even if you are not a leader. If you have good social skills, it will improve how you communicate with others, making you a better leader in the process. If you are a leader, it will improve how you will be perceived by those under you.

Empathy

Empathy is very important to emotional intelligence; empathy is the ability to understand the feelings of others. However, empathy goes beyond understanding the emotions and feelings of others. Your response to those emotions is just as important as knowing what they are feeling. For example, if you come across a friend who just lost someone, you should pay extra attention to them, do things that can improve their spirits, and help alleviate other burdens. However, all Men should learn how to control their emotions, but you should also learn how to tolerate people by understanding their emotions. It is okay to indulge your friends and families when they are sad or depressed. This behavior will help you in all forms of relationships because empathy allows you to see things how others see them. Alpha Males are seen as leaders, and if you want to be the leader, you must have empathy. Empathy is the bedrock of leadership as it gives you a solid understanding of how people work. If you are able to empathize with others, people will respect you, and it will improve your social skills. This principle is useful in your relationships, where most times they are power dynamics. This is very important in a workplace environment, and it will improve how you react with others daily.

Motivation

Emotionally intelligent Men have a drive that comes from within. They understand that working towards goals because of the passion they derive from doing it is more rewarding. They have a desire to work for the things that they want persistently and with energy. Emotionally intelligent Men are filled with vigor and the desire to fulfill personal goals instead of being motivated by extrinsic rewards like money and fame. The inner motivation that they have is not limited to their personal needs, and they also like to assist others in becoming successful.

How To Use Emotional Intelligence

Emotional intelligence has a huge effect on different parts of our lives. If you want to enjoy the benefits and the power that comes along with it, you must know how to use it. Some of the ways that Alpha Males use emotional intelligence are listed below;

Assertive communication

All human beings during the course of their lives will have both positive and negative feelings, but how these feelings are communicated differs. It is important to know how to communicate what you are feeling to people around you, and if you're an emotionally intelligent Man, you do this by expressing your feelings directly without disrespecting others. If you want to develop emotional intelligence, you must pay attention to your feelings, be honest with what you are feeling, and understand what those feelings are when you've analyzed if they're based on your previous experiences. Think about your reactions in previous situations and think of how you can improve your reactions by meditation. You should only react with a clear mind. Your reactions should not be too aggressive or passive. For example, if your boss says something that you do not like, ensure that you settle those feelings inwardly before you react. This method of reaction has helped me convey my feelings without being too aggressive. I have also discovered that when I react this way, those feelings are properly understood and get better reactions.

Focus on your response

There would be situations in your life where people would annoy you, or things might not go your way which could lead to outbursts. You will also experience conflicts whether you want it or not. During these moments, the common human reaction would be for you to show feelings of anger or display emotional outbursts. This occurs a lot in relationships. Your partner could start saying negative things about you. I have had partners who have said hurtful things when angry. I have heard some say the sex is not even good; their ex-boyfriend is a better Man, your jokes are not even funny, you do not deserve to be loved, etc. Hearing these things being said about you is never cool, but I have always managed to *keep* my cool. (Did you get the pun?!) However, if you want to be an Alpha Male, you must not behave like everyone does or expects. Instead of resorting to anger and emotional outbursts, channel your emotional intelligence into staying calm. An emotionally intelligent Man knows how to maintain composure during stressful situations. Use your emotional intelligence to keep your emotions under check and avoid making impulsive decisions that often result in bigger problems. As an Alpha Male, you should know that in stressful situations, the goal is not to display superiority unless it is the only solution. The goal is resolution, and you should make a conscious effort to align your words and actions towards resolution.

Active listening skills

As I mentioned earlier in this chapter, it is easy to identify an emotionally intelligent Man. This is because they have some traits that are particular to them. You can know them from the way they converse with others, and an emotionally intelligent Man is not always the loudest. They do not need to shout at the top of their voices, drowning out the voice of others, for people to understand them. Instead of shouting, they listen for clarity and wait their turn before they talk. If you want people to know you as an emotionally intelligent individual, you must ensure you understand what is being said before you respond. Alpha Males use their emotional intelligence to understand verbal and non-verbal details of any conversation before they talk. When you take time to understand others, it prevents disagreements and makes others respect and listen to you. Since I started paying attention and listening to my girlfriend, I found that I have prevented many disagreements. You must learn to listen even if it does not interest you. I have listened to several stories about Tom, Ben, and Sandra, who are always disturbing my girlfriend at work. In fact, I could write a book about each one of them. Even though most of the stories are boring, they have been helpful.

Positivity

Your attitude plays a huge role in how people view and respond to you. The kind of attitude that you show impacts the reaction of others to you; if you have a negative attitude, it will easily affect others, as well as people around you. Emotionally intelligent Men understand the effect of their attitude on others and ensure that they guard their attitude accordingly. Use your emotional intelligence to understand what can improve your attitude and ensure that you do it daily so that you can always have a positive approach. Your attitude depends on you, and it can be controlled by using emotional intelligence. Men who exude positivity in tough situations are often Alpha Males because it's one of their characteristics.

Sociable

Emotional intelligence will also affect your social skills, and emotionally intelligent Men have good social skills. These social skills improve their relationships. They often smile a lot. However, having good social skills does not mean you should always smile. Use your emotional intelligence to understand and decide on what should be the best response in each situation. Alpha Males should be able to channel their emotional intelligence into their interpersonal and social skills because it will make them come over as approachable. There are no downsides to having good social skills, and it allows you to have more influence over others. One of the areas of good social skills is communication, and you should be able to communicate clearly, both verbally and nonverbally.

Benefits Of Emotional Intelligence

You should have no doubts about how emotional intelligence can be beneficial to Men or how it can help you in different aspects of your life. Emotions are a vital aspect of human beings, and the ability to influence your personal emotions and the emotions of others gives you power. Some benefits of the power of emotional intelligence to Alpha Men will be explained below;

Improves leadership skills

Alpha Males are often leaders, and the ability of a leader depends on his team. A leader is only as good as his team allows. If you want your team to improve, you must be able to influence them to become better. There are many ways to influence people, but you can also use emotional intelligence as a power to influence others. Great leaders have some similar features, and one of those features is that they understand the people they are leading. Emotional intelligence allows you to know people under you, relate with them, and know how they work. This creates a good leadership atmosphere, and your followers or team members will be ready to work for you. When you have a relationship with people under you, you will be able to motivate and inspire them to do more. This understanding will help you become a better leader as you lead your team in the right direction.

React well to changes

Despite the fact that change is the only constant thing in life, many of us still struggle with it. Sometimes those changes become sources of anger and frustration. Some Men stop showing empathy when they are faced with changes. However, emotionally intelligent Men who understand their emotions and how they affect others will successfully manage the feelings that come with change. Such feelings could be stress and anxiety, and when you can manage these feelings, people will trust you and be confident in your abilities. This will also make others respect you and increase your influence. The increase in influence you enjoy is because of the power of emotional intelligence.

Productivity

Not only does emotional intelligence help you to manage stressful situations successfully, but it will also help you to retain your focus and not be derailed by the negative emotions of others. When you are able to manage others and also help them resolve matters during heated exchanges, your productivity will increase. It is not only products that will increase. The relationship that you have forged using emotional intelligence with your team members will also help them flourish.

Improve relationships

The type of relationship that you have is a direct reflection of how much you respect each other. If you want to have a successful relationship with your family, friends, associates, boss, and partner, you need emotional intelligence. One unavoidable truth about relationships is that there will be conflicts, and your ability to manage those conflicts will determine the duration of your relationship. Emotional intelligence teaches you how to build and maintain effective relationships. Relationships with people require you to have more emotional intelligence than IQ. Emotional intelligence will help you keep emotions in check and not react poorly in conflicts. For instance, when a partner moves in with you, the first few weeks could be challenging as you get to know things they do and vice-versa. Many relationships end in that first week, not because they do not love each other, but because they could not live together. Most times, this occurs as a result of low emotional intelligence; couples start picking fights unnecessarily. However, this could help you become stronger if you can get through it, but people with low emotional intelligence who are not in control of their emotions often can't handle it. During these rows, they might say hurtful things out of anger which can cause irredeemable damage. But Men who have the power of emotional intelligence will be able to handle changes that come in relationships and have the social skills to respond appropriately. Emotionally intelligent Men also tend to listen more to partners even if the partner shares negative thoughts or feelings. Alpha Males must have the emotional intelligence to navigate the waters of those relationships. Power does not only come from physical dominance. The type of relationship you keep also gives you power.

How To Develop Emotional Intelligence

The impact of emotional intelligence on human lives cannot be overstated. Emotional intelligence affects the quality of individual lives because its effect can be felt in relationships and behaviors. During the course of a day, we will be faced with important decisions; sometimes, these decisions have great impacts on how our lives turn out. There are many factors that can affect our decisions, but if you want to be able to make the right choices, you must develop your emotional intelligence. Below are some things that can help improve the emotional intelligence of an Alpha Male.

Improve self-awareness

Alpha Males always strive for improvement all round, especially the vital parts of human lives such as identifying emotions. If you want to improve on your ability to identify your personal emotions and how they affect people around you, you should practice mindfulness. Mindfulness is an ability that all humans can have but often do not use because they are not willing to work for it. This ability makes you aware of your present situation without judgment or being overwhelmed. You can improve this ability by meditation. You can take some moments daily to reminisce on your reactions throughout the day and create time for reflection on those reactions. During your meditation, look inward and consider what your strengths and weaknesses are because you will only be able to improve your weakness when you know them.

Know your triggers

Alpha Males should not let anyone or anything determine their reaction. Alpha Males are always in charge of every aspect of their lives, be it mental, emotional, and psychological. Emotional intelligence deals with the ability to manage emotions. Most changes in emotions occur as a result of triggers. For example, if you touch something hot, your reaction will be to remove your hand; the trigger is the heat. There are some things that cause a change in our emotions, and sometimes those changes are bad. You will be able to manage your emotions better if you know the things that can trigger a change of emotion. During your meditation, think about what triggered your reactions. Once you identify them, you can isolate, anticipate, and control different parts of interactions where they occur. When you are analyzing your triggers, you might deduce that sometimes words or actions that made you feel offended could be genuine attempts to help. For example, if you have a friend that speaks bluntly and this gets you offended, you can avoid getting angry by limiting situations that could cause him to say the things you do not like.

Recognize and celebrate positive emotions

If you want to radiate positivity frequently as an Alpha Male should, you must take time out to do things that generate positive emotions. These things do not have to be expensive, like going to the Caribbean for a weekend or skydiving each day. You can generate positive emotions from past happy memories, and you can carry out activities that make you feel good about yourself, such as being kind and nice. When you do such activities, ensure you reward yourself. This idea comes from the school of thought that an influx of positive emotions puts you in a stronger place to control negative emotions when they come. The positivity radiating inwards makes you more resilient to negative emotions.

Attention

If you want to have a better understanding of others, you must pay attention to their feelings. You can do this by listening to and understanding what they are trying to tell you verbally and nonverbally. If you want to have good social skills, you must be able to understand the body language of people around you. Ensure that before you respond, you gather the facts and pay attention to their feelings before you deliver a response. Adequate attention will improve your relationship with others, and you will improve the way you react to others.

In this chapter, I have explained what emotional intelligence entails and the principles behind this law of power. The power provided by this law is also useful, and I have explained how Men can use it. The power to influence emotions is beneficial to Alpha Males who are ready to employ it. Not all Men are born with this power, but you can learn it; this chapter also provides ways that Alpha Males can use to develop this power they now have.

CONCLUSION

YOU HAVE NOW FINISHED READING this book about the seven laws of power. You should know how those laws can help you become an Alpha Male. By now, you should know the meaning of each law of power and how you can use it. You should also know the benefits that you will enjoy from using each law of power in different spheres of your life, and how power can be abused.

However, not everyone who knows how to use this power will use it because of fear. Although one of the things that comes with being an Alpha power is courage, before you become an Alpha Male, you must act like one. What this means is that you will be courageous and start practicing what you have read.

Taking that bold decision is the first decision you will make on the journey towards becoming an Alpha Man. You can use the book as reference material to guide you on further decisions. This book has provided examples that have helped Men accrue much power, and by doing so, they've vastly improved their lifestyles. Why shouldn't this be you? There's no reason on earth why not. The kind of impact this book will have on you depends solely on you. I sincerely wish you the greatest of fortune on your quest.

201 Positive Affirmations For Alpha Males

DESCRIPTION

These affirmations are designed to improve your personal magnetism, harmonize your brain's abilities, and help your subconscious mind to change your unconscious beliefs.

Read these powerful affirmations for 21 days in a row and watch your life and how you think of yourself begin to transform around you.

Your dominant thoughts create your reality.

The brain is made up of the conscious and the subconscious mind. 90-95% of our everyday life is the result of our subconscious mind being programmed. It controls everything from breathing to cell repair, hair growth to our heartbeat. We all have subconscious beliefs and habits that prevent us from living out our true potential. To change old beliefs, we must replace them with new ones.

Use these affirmations to reprogram your subconscious mind. Read them for at least 21 days/nights in a row as you're in bed falling asleep. When reading, try to imagine yourself as your ideal version, and feel the emotions of how it would be if you were already that ideal version.

50 Positive Affirmations For Success

1. I am focused and never quit
2. I am committed to maximizing my success
3. A challenge brings out the best in me
4. If I am to fail, I will fail forward
5. My dreams are there to achieve
6. My confidence has no limit
7. I will do what it takes to achieve my goals
8. I will seize every opportunity presented to me
9. I am prepared to go the extra mile
10. Hard work fulfills me
11. Success comes naturally to me
12. Success is my driving force
13. I love what I do
14. I believe in myself
15. I'm worthy of success
16. I choose what I become
17. I deserve success
18. I excel in all that I do
19. I set high standards for myself
20. I am focused

21. I am patient

22. I trust the universe

23. I respect myself

24. I will be great

25. I have limitless potential

26. I have an opportunity

27. I will do whatever it takes

28. Nothing can stop me

29. I will achieve my goals

30. I see my goal clearly

31. I am determined

32. I see challenges as opportunities for growth

33. I am the architect of my life

34. I'm a magnet for success

35. I'm right where I need to be

36. I live my life without fear

37. I feel things falling into place

38. I like myself

39. Success is second nature to me

40. Mistakes are a stepping stone to success

41. I am proud of my success

42. I think only of success

43. All problems have a solution

44. I am in charge of my life

45. My power comes from within me

46. I find inspiration easily

47. Consistency is key to my success

48. Everything I touch is a success

49. I am persistent

50. Life is full of choices. I choose success

51 Positive Affirmations For Wealth

1. Money comes to me easily
2. I attract money
3. My mind is focused on wealth
4. Every day, I am becoming richer
5. My actions lead to prosperity
6. Prosperity is my birthright
7. I enjoy the rewards of working
8. I appreciate the value of things
9. I radiate positivity
10. My attitude attracts wealth
11. I can provide for my family
12. Money allows me to help people
13. Fortune favors me
14. I will become financially abundant
15. I am receptive to wealth and success
16. My life is filled with riches
17. I will achieve my financial desires
18. I am grateful for my wealth
19. My success is predetermined
20. I am abundant

21. Success leads to wealth and I am successful
22. I am a wealth magnet
23. I attract people who will help me in achieving wealth
24. I am highly driven
25. I will become financially free
26. I choose to be wealthy
27. My energy is aligned with wealth
28. I am wealth
29. Money comes to me in expected and unexpected ways
30. I deserve wealth
31. Money always finds its way to me
32. The universe serves my best interests
33. I always have enough
34. I am worth the money
35. I love luxury
36. I am blessed with money
37. I deserve to live a life of luxury
38. My wallet is overflowing with money
39. I feel rich
40. My prosperity is unlimited
41. Money is great
42. I am financially secure

43. I attract wealth and prosperity

44. I am happy, healthy, and wealthy

45. I always have opportunities to make more money

46. I attract money, love, and happiness wherever I go

47. I welcome unlimited income into my life

48. I am destined to be wealthy

49. It's my choice as to how much money I make

50. I have an endless supply of cash

51. Today is a day of amazing good fortune

25 Positive Affirmations For Alpha Male Mindset

1. I embrace my masculinity

2. I view myself as a strong and capable Man

3. I feel strong and confident, regardless of the situation

4. I become stronger and more beautiful every day

5. I am a natural leader and easily accomplish my goals

6. My greatest weapon is my optimism

7. I have the courage to wear whatever I want

8. Women naturally gravitate towards me

9. I am in love with my true self

10. I deserve the love of a strong woman/Man

11. Confidence comes naturally to me

12. I am dominant

13. I am totally secure in myself

14. When I speak, I carry authority

15. I can take the lead in any social situation

16. I was born to be an Alpha Male

17. Assertiveness and dominance come naturally to me

18. I enjoy being a leader

19. I am highly respected

20. It's OK to be strong, both mentally and physically

21. I am proud to be a Man
22. Today, I will start loving myself more
23. I will surround myself with other positive, confident Men
24. I will continue to strengthen my Alpha traits
25. Others look up to my strength of character

25 Positive Affirmations For Dealing With Depression

1. Life is beautiful

2. I feel grateful to be alive

3. I am in charge of how I feel and today I will feel happy

4. I forgive myself for my past mistakes. Every new day is an opportunity to start over

5. I will overcome and get through any feelings of sadness

6. My mind is powerful. When I fill it with positive thoughts, my life will begin to change.

7. I am brave

8. I have enthusiasm for life

9. I will not focus on what hurts me. I will focus on what brings me joy

10. I will keep going and I will grow stronger

11. It is in my power to be happy

12. This, too, shall pass

13. I deserve to be happy

14. I am grateful for the good things in my life

15. I love myself

16. More and more, I can see the beauty of my own being

17. I am worthy of love and happiness

18. I will not let myself become discouraged

19. I can find beauty in even the smallest things

20. I'm OK with where I am right now

21. I love myself

22. Hard times offer me opportunities to grow

23. I find and enjoy the simple pleasures life has to offer

24. Life wants the best for me

25. I will not judge myself negatively

25 Positive Affirmations For Men: Anxiety

1. I am safe and loved

2. I have faith that everything will work out in the end

3. What I want is already here or on its way

4. I appreciate everything I have

5. As I let go of things, the better I feel

6. I breathe in relaxation, I breathe out the tension

7. I am free of anything that will weigh me down

8. Life is beautiful, wonderful, and peaceful

9. I am mentally strong and don't take things personally

10. I attract positive energy into my mind and body

11. I attract positive and confident people into my life

12. I accept myself for who I am

13. I am cool, calm, and collected

14. Worry and anxiety will not change my circumstances. Only positive actions and thoughts can

15. Happiness and joy flow easily to me

16. I have confidence in myself and my abilities

17. Success will be the force that drives me

18. I will speak with confidence

19. I do not fear to be wrong

20. When I put my mind to something, I am unstoppable

21. Happiness is within my grasp

22. I accept and love myself for who I am

23. I am ready to take on any challenge

24. I become stronger and more confident every day

25. I am in complete control of my anxiety

25 Positive Affirmations To Start Off Your Day

1. Every time I wake up, I am grateful to be alive
2. Today, I will focus only on positive thoughts and energy
3. Today, I will finish all my tasks with joy
4. Each day is filled with abundance and joy
5. I will go to sleep a better person than I am at this moment
6. Good energy flows through me
7. Today, I will manifest new opportunities
8. I am full of ideas
9. I will make the most out of today
10. Today could be one of the best days in my life
11. My happiness grows stronger every day
12. I am calm and at peace
13. I choose to do great things today
14. I will enjoy everything today has to offer
15. I am ready to take on the day
16. Today, I will be smarter, kinder, and wiser
17. I honor all my responsibilities
18. I trust the process that is life
19. I manifest abundance easily
20. I will become a better version of myself today

21. I will start each day with a grateful heart

22. The world needs my energy and ideas

23. No matter what happened the day before, I will get up, show up, and never give up

24. I am positive and will attract good things in my direction

25. Today, I will worry less and smile more

ALPHA MALE BIBLE

Charisma, Psychology of Attraction, Charm.
Art of Confidence, Self-Hypnosis, Meditation.
Art of Body Language, Eye Contact, Small Talk.
Habits & Self-Discipline of a Real Alpha Man.

SEAN WAYNE

ALPHA MALE DATING
The Essential Playbook

**Single → Engaged → Married (If You Want).
Love Hypnosis, Law of Attraction,
Art of Seduction, Intimacy in Bed.
Attract Women as an Irresistible Alpha Man.**

SUPREME ALPHA MALE BIBLE
The 1ne

**Empath & Psychic Abilities Power.
Success Mindset, Psychology, Confidence.
Win Friends & Influence People.
Hypnosis, Body Language, Atomic Habits.
Dating: The Secret.**

★★★

I Would Appreciate It if You Left a Review,
It's Very Important.

★★★

f SEAN WAYNE

@

mr.sean.wayne.author@gmail.com